W9-APK-923

Jesus told
me to... Tell
Them
I am
Coming

The personal testimony of a physician concerning his relationship with a personal Saviour, who loves, heals, and recreates, in order to commission His children to invite others to share His abundant life and eternal joy, here and in heaven, with the Living God who is about to return in clouds, to meet them in person!

RICHARD E. EBY

Jesus told me to... Tell Them I am Coming

SPIRE BOOKS

Fleming H. Revell
A Division of Baker Book House Co
Grand Rapids, Michigan 49516

Library of Congress Cataloging-in-Publication Data

Eby, Richard E.
    Tell them I am coming.

    1. Eby, Richard E.   2. Christian biography—
United States.   3. Physicians—United States—
Biography.   I. Title.
BR1725.E25A37   248.2   80-41
ISBN 0-8007-8496-0

A Spire Book
Copyright © 1980 by Richard E. Eby
Spire Books are published by Fleming H. Revell
a division of Baker Book House Company
P.O. Box 6287, Grand Rapids, Michigan 49516-6287
All rights reserved

Twelfth printing, November 1996

Printed in the United States of America

TO the hosts of earthly friends
and ministering angels, whose
combined prayers and continu-
ing protection have interceded
to permit us to share the
indescribable joy in Jesus, the
matchless grace of God, and the
indwelling of the Spirit

Dear Partner:

We are so pleased to present this latest work of Dr. Richard Eby to you with the prayer that it will bring many of your loved ones to Christ. The message of this book was given to Dr. Eby from the heart of Lazarus' Tomb in Bethany. "Tell them, tell them, tell them, that I am coming soon," were the very words of Jesus to each of us through Dr. Eby. We pray that you will join the great chorus of voices that are being raised up by the Holy Spirit that Jesus is coming soon!

Jan and I appreciate your love and support for the continuance of this great Television ministry.

Yours to reach the yet unreached,

Paul F. Crouch
Founder/President

Contents

Preface

Jesus told me a short time ago, "There is yet a little time, but very little." He abolished all doubt about His coming: "Behold, I come quickly."

The Holy Scriptures and the Holy Spirit proclaim His reasons for such a miracle: "I love you."

Now, in our generation, Jesus is about to fulfill His greatest promise for us: "I will come again and receive you unto Myself."

The following story is my testimony of His love for me and others, as He reveals His plan and place for us in Him. He touched me. I want Him to touch you. You are equally precious to Him.

He bids us: "Come!"

Foreword

September 7, 1979

The first words I heard from Richard Eby were: "For a Christian, there is no such thing as death."

What a strange thing for a medical doctor to say, who lives with death every day. But as his fascinating story unfolded in the church meeting in West Covina—of a tragic fall, a broken body, dead on arrival, a breathtaking glimpse of paradise, visions too wondrous to describe— Jan and I sensed that this was from God, and should be shared with television audiences around the world.

Since then, Dr. Eby and his vivacious wife, Maybelle, have shared their testimonies many times over the Trinity Broadcasting Network's prime-time "Praise the Lord" programs. Each time, hundreds of souls have been gripped with the reality of life after death and have committed their lives to the Lord Jesus Christ!

The Ebys have accompanied our TBN Missions Team to Haiti, Guatemala, Puerto Rico, Korea, Hong Kong, Indonesia, Israel, and Hawaii—sharing the miracles described in his book *Caught Up Into Paradise*. In every country, the result has been the same—hundreds giving their lives to Jesus, at altars, in auditoriums, in the open-air stadiums, even on a boat in Hong Kong harbor'

Jan and I count Dr. and Mrs. Eby among our closest and dearest friends and commend this latest book without reservation. It is calling to God's children to come and set themselves apart for that glorious moment when we will share an "out of this world experience" as we are forever united with our King of Kings and Lord of Lords.

> Paul F. Crouch
> President
> Trinity Broadcasting Network

August 22, 1979

One of the most popular guests ever on "The 700 Club" was Dr. Richard Eby, the California physician who accidentally died and visited paradise, then returned to earth.

Because of the tremendous flood of letters about his testimony, I asked Dr. Eby to come here again. The things he shared are so important that I want to make sure you know about them.

Years after his accident, Dr. Eby actually saw Jesus appear in human form. Jesus assured him He is coming back to earth "in a moment's time," and Dr. Eby will not die again before it happens. What striking news for a man already in his sixties to have heard! With compassion for a lost world, Jesus said, "Tell them, tell them, tell them."

When Jesus repeats something three times, it is so that no one can fail to understand. His urgent message is for you and me, too. We must "tell them, tell them, tell them!"

Your brother in Christ,
Pat Robertson
President, Christian
Broadcasting Network

Acknowledgments

Appreciation is expressed to the ministers and Christian laymen, who, by sharing with us their pulpits, podiums, television and radio programs, have enabled us to witness more effectively about God's limitless love for lost sheep, His yearning for their return, and His promise to come for them soon.

We especially thank our great Christian TV networks, under the anointed leadership of saints such as Paul and Jan and Jim and Pat and David, for enriching our lives through their friendship and prayers.

Jesus, we thank You for all these!

Introduction—
Come Home, Children

> And a voice came out of the throne, saying,
> Praise our God, all ye his servants, and ye that
> fear him, both small and great. And I heard as it
> were the voice of a great multitude, and as the
> voice of many waters, and as the voice of mighty
> thunderings, saying, Alleluia: for the Lord God
> omnipotent reigneth. Let us be glad and rejoice,
> and give honour to him: for the marriage of the
> Lamb is come, and his wife hath made herself
> ready . . . . And he saith unto me, Write, Blessed
> are they which are called unto the marriage sup-
> per of the Lamb. And he saith unto me, These are
> the true sayings of God.
>
> Revelation 19:5–7, 9

FOR SHEER JOY, little can compare in the life of a child with mother's voice, calling from home's doorway, "Come home, children!"

It means so many things to a little heart and a hungry tummy! I can remember it well, even after half a century. Mother's voice would carry down to the dock, where brother and I would be in a life-and-death contest to see

17

who could catch the most crayfish before the evening
shadows stopped our fun. Or we might be on hands and
knees in a wild-strawberry patch, seeking goodies (most
of them mashed into our clothing) when the call came
that supper was ready.

Later on, it meant that we could stop worming the to-
mato plants or weeding the asparagus patch or picking
the Yellow Transparent apples that squashed like a sack
of water when dropped. Or it meant that the sweaty
chore of mowing the hillside lawn in the August heat of
the Berkshire Hills could halt, or that the Latin lesson
could be interrupted.

"Supper's ready" really meant "Somebody loves you."
It meant that no matter how tired mother felt, she had
been busy peeling potatoes, baking beans, or mixing bat-
ter for a strawberry shortcake—just because she loved us.
And even though her back ached from carrying the wood
up from the basement to keep the oven hot, we would
never hear her complain. Her husband and boys came
first.

"Supper's ready" also meant the completion of a task
that had required so much planning. The "supermarket"
consisted of the vegetable cellar next to the coal bin in the
basement. Nothing came out unless something went in!
That meant weeks of spading the garden, sowing seeds,
pulling weeds, fighting cutworms. It meant picking and
canning—hours over a hot stove, with its steaming gal-
vanized tub full of Mason jars and lids being sterilized. It
meant that mother's hands were red and raw much of the
time from husking, peeling, paring, handling hot jars, and
screwing on their boiling-hot lids.

"Supper's ready" meant that the months of planning had worked. It meant that the rain and sleet and snow that stopped the outdoor life from growing could not prevent mother from seeing her family grow. It meant that she and dad had looked much further ahead than we children could and had made provision for a day of need.

Beyond that, suppertime was a reward. We knew it would happen every evening. Mom would take off her apron; dad would remove his starched, button-on collar when he came from work; we boys would stomp off the mud from our year-old shoes and leave them on the rear stoop. The smells in the kitchen were so good that it was hard to wait for the blessing, but it made things taste better, somehow, to say thank You in advance.

Suppertime was something special. There was nothing to distract us from getting to know one another. Mother was in no hurry to do the dishes in the hot water at the end of the wood stove. Dad was happy to change the pace of the day, from frenzied inventing at General Electric to the leisure of a suppertime with his family. And we boys saw no point in rushing back to numbers or history or Latin.

Besides, we had sneaked "secrets" under each plate as we sat down! Of course, no one dared look until dessert was over, then we all looked. On each scrap of paper was a question, sometimes two. Each was addressed to one of us. With an expectant hush, we would look around, to see who would lead off. Usually, it was Dad—he was the wisest. Of course Mother always knew what we really meant! Then we boys would finish the conference by answering the questions under our plates: "Did you learn something new today?" "When will you have time to go fishing next?" "Do the raspberries need mulching?" "How is the music lesson coming along?" We felt a mile high as we took off to our studies.

It has taken God a large part of eternity to prepare the universe and His children for that moment when "the Voice out of the throne" can announce, "Supper's ready."

Can you imagine the glad house in heaven right now, as the angels rush around on tiptoe, smoothing the snow white tablecloths, setting out the golden service, and placing the name cards on the banquet table? Furtively they glance toward the throne to see whether they can be prepared in time. They already hear the rumbling voices of the great multitude approaching in the distance, exalting over the impending blessing! Everything is happening so fast, they notice.

What planning it has taken! What love! What sacrifice! What unbelievable mercy! And above all, what patience! Even the angels marvel that Jesus would have waited so long for this Marriage Supper of the Lamb!

Soon He will be sitting down with His family. At long last, He can show them, *in person*, that He is the Conqueror. He can break bread and share secrets with them. He can rest after the battles of those earthly days. His unsearchable provisions for His children can be distributed to His joint heirs. He can love them with a new intensity because, through this Marriage Supper, they have become *one*!

The stories that follow, in this account of our personal

experiences in Jesus' pre-Supper generation, are meant to illustrate how our God is fitting together all the pieces in His great plan.

His Spirit is being poured out anew, as never before. His banquet table is being set. His Word is being carried to the uttermost parts, in methods and amounts never previously possible until He revealed modern science for believers to use.

There can be nothing more exciting than living in these days—nothing except hearing Him say, "I am coming. Supper's ready!"

Lazarus, Come Forth

Jesus said unto her, I am the resurrection, and
the life: he that believeth in me, though he were
dead, yet shall he live . . . . Believeth thou this? . . .
And when he thus had spoken, he cried with a
loud voice, Lazarus, come forth.

John 11: 25, 26, 43

IF EVERYONE KNEW that Jesus is the Resurrection of both
the body and the soul, heaven could and would be here,
now! The angels would be ecstatic, and I would not be
taking time to tell you about Jesus' love for us. Instead,
the Creator has had to spend an eternity to prepare this
resurrection for you and me.

Perhaps you will find this truth hard to believe. So did
many eyewitnesses of Jesus' miracles. They spat at Him
and scoffed in His presence. They tried to kill Him on a
tree. But He lives today! And because He lives, a few
years ago, Jesus asked me to reveal to people what He
showed and told me in Lazarus's tomb. Let me tell you
how it came about: first, His encounter with Lazarus, then
with me.

Bethany, A.D. 33

Springtime had crept northward up the Jordan Valley
to the east, warming the waters and fattening the fruits on

23

the laden branches. A spirit of excitement hung over the shores of Galilee, where growing numbers of curious travelers were assembling from villages in the hills. There was more in the air than the aroma of ripening figs and citrus. Something special was happening.

The milling crowd had collected rapidly around a group absorbed in the street preaching of their leader, a man with the dialect of a Nazarene. He was comely, calm, and He made good sense. He talked about Jehovah's promises so knowledgeably that many believed Him to be a prophet. Some whispered, "Perhaps, the Messiah?" Others turned away, more interested in the fresh fruit or righteous rituals at the synagogue.

Abruptly, a commotion and shouting interrupted the preacher. With robes flapping against the flanks of a sweating donkey, a dusty-eyed courier whipped his tiring beast through the ranks of listeners, almost knocking Jesus into Peter. "Rabboni," he gasped, "Your friend Lazarus of Bethany is sick unto death! Mary and Martha need You there today!" The crowd hushed. After all, Bethany was across the wilderness and up that long, dangerous road to Jerusalem, where it would be like giving one's life for a friend to travel in the heat.

Jesus was unperturbed: ". . . This sickness is not unto death, but for the glory of God . . ." (John 11:4). With a wave of His hand, He bade the bewildered rider to carry His answer back to Bethany: "I will return from the Jordan in a few days."

The rest of the story is well known. The frightened but faithful disciples went with Jesus, fearing that the restless mobs would stone them to death enroute. The tears of a disappointed Mary and Martha bathed the heavy stone placed across the cave's mouth, while Lazarus's body inside began to rot.

When Jesus reached Bethany, He found that Martha's faith had failed her, even in His presence. When He asked her, "Believeth thou, that he that believeth in Me, though he were dead, yet shall live?" she repeated her creed, instead of answering His question. Mary rushed to meet Him with her cry of disappointment: "Lord, if Thou hadst been here. . . ." How Jesus groaned to hear the spectators' murmurs about a man who could open blind eyes but could not prevent a death!

Jesus looked up and read His Father's mind: "Remember, Son, when We made man? You blew the breath of life into him then. For My glory do it again!"

Jesus shouted, "Thank You, Father! Lazarus, come forth!" Mary and Martha and the disciples and the multitude *saw* the glory of God, and many believed.

Bethany, A.D. 1977

Nineteen centuries later, I found Jesus again in Bethany. My wife and I, along with 250 excited partners, were touring the sacred sites of Israel with our Trinity Broadcasting Network hosts, Paul and Jan Crouch. To some of our group, Jesus was still just a historical figure. By the tour's end, they would know Him as a living Saviour, their new Source of abundant life! For some of us, He was already a longtime Companion and Healer.

From the hewn-stone entrance to the traditional site of Lazarus's tomb, we pick our way down a curving tunnel, over worn steps, till we reach the mourning room.

In 1979, two years later, Dr. Eby revisits the tunnel of stone leading from the mourning room to Lazarus's tomb. This time it is lighted!

As our bus pulled away from the Old City's walls where the very stones seemed to be crying out their messages of the reality of resurrection, I had no idea that Jesus was preparing a special event for me that day. Minutes later, we halted at a hillside pathway in Bethany. The guide led us up the incline, past the ancient, ornate Church of the Resurrection, while little children thrust souvenirs in our faces. "Three fo' a dollah," they shouted. At the top, we stopped to read the sign above the hewn-stone entrance: St. Lazarus Tomb

Down a curving tunnel, over worn stone steps, we picked our way to the mourning room, two stories below the present ground level. I slid down the last three steps, through the boy-sized tunnel into the tomb, and stood up.

Two ladies were there already. I noted the eight-foot-square sepulcher, with its arched ceiling and single light bulb, its cold walls, and the muted sounds of their voices and rustling clothes and shoes.

Through my mind rushed the history of this tomb, where a "rotting," wrapped Lazarus had heard a shout, and felt himself come alive and lifted through the door-way, wrappings and all; how he had found himself standing in the blinding sunlight while excited hands un-bound him from the graveclothes before the multitude of gaping faces and how Jesus had exclaimed. "Thank You, Father, for hearing Me, that they may see Your glory!"

Suddenly, the light went out! The ladies gave muffled screams and my heart skipped a beat. Being two stories underground in pitch-black isolation was disturbing! I assumed a fuse had blown, and I heard myself reflexly reassure the women: "Please, ladies, pray and praise. It's just the fuse."

"My Son"

Then the *Miracle*! I did not even have time to join them in a prayer. Instead, I felt instantly alone in the total darkness. There was not a rustle or a sound of breathing from the ladies. They were gone as far as I could determine. I dropped to the ground and groped for the exit tunnel. I was alone! But only for an instant. Suddenly, beside me stood a man! In my kneeling posture I sensed, then saw a person pressing against me on my right side. First, I saw the toes protruding from the flowing robe; then as I panned upward, the golden sash, beautifully muscled arms, shoulder-length, light golden hair. The hands were hidden: one on my left shoulder, the other between the gown and the cold stone wall. To see His face, I looked upward; He was six feet tall or more, and looking downward into my face! Portions of His beard and mustache were missing. (I was not surprised.) His hair was illuminated.

I knew instantly that He was my Lord. Without a shadow of doubt, I knew also that in His presence I again had the *mind* of Christ which He had shared with me five years before this, when He spoke with me in heaven. Though I had never before seen my Saviour's face, He was telling me directly upon my mind (with which I was now seeing Him) that I was truly *with* Him and *in* Him there in the tomb.

The royalty of that face! How can I describe its sovereignty, its compassion, its overwhelming look of righteousness? In it I saw the justice of our Intercessor, the joy of our Healer, the humility of His Father's Faithful Servant. I saw a display of meekness without weakness, of limitless power with infinite gentleness and those penetrating eyes, emitting a radiance of indescribably limitless love! Nothing can be compared with the eyes of our God. They held me spellbound. I actually *saw* the truth of His claim that "Greater love hath no man." I knew He was looking at me and through me with the same forgiveness and love which He showers upon all Doubting Thomases.

This I noted in the fraction of a second, and I saw a slight frown of concern form on His face like a cloud of sadness. He quickly spoke two words in English: "My son!" Then He continued with the same lightning-fast language we had used during my time in heaven.

"I must show you hell, but just for two minutes! I have already shown you heaven. I want you to *tell them, tell them, tell them.*"

How it must have hurt Him to send me into hell, even for two short minutes! No wonder He frowned at the thought: He had been there! He had once told His disciples to ask His Father to "deliver us from the evil one." If it weren't that He already had the keys to hell and death in His right hand there in the tomb, He would not have sent me to Satan's home to experience the horrors of a lost soul. Jesus knew He could bring me back, because He had already broken the power of Satan to bind a child of God!

My Orders

As though in shock, I stood stock-still, wondering what I should "tell them." He already knew my thoughts and was answering me at a million words a second. I will try to summarize His command to me.

"You must tell them that I gave them a will when I created them. They must make a choice between Me or My adversary, Satan. Man cannot live without a master; his soul is made to worship someone. Tell them I am a gentleman; I will never override their free will. I created them to be free to choose, because I would not create anyone to be a slave. Satan offers them the security of slavery, but his wages are death. I offer them freedom and the righteousness of My Father in heaven, where our gift of love and life is eternal."

In seconds, Jesus had transmitted to me volumes of spiritual data, bypassing my ears and brain which would have been far too sluggish to receive His instructions. For emphasis He repeated insistently: *"Tell them. Tell them. Tell them.* Tell them how much I love them! I left heaven to come and die for them. I had to destroy the works of the devil so My children could be freed! I arose to present them blameless before My Father in heaven! Tell them they can choose life with Me—all for free. I paid the price. Tell them they will have the unsearchable riches that My Father has prepared for them. They can choose to belong to the family of God. They can reign with Me as kings and priests through the ages. I will send them My Spirit. I will heal their infirmities. I will forgive their sins. Tell them I took their place on My cross!" At this He shuddered.

"Tell them," He continued, "My grace is sufficient for them. It is My gift of love. They cannot earn it by their works. I finished all the work and waiting on the cross. All they must do is receive Me into their hearts and accept me as their Way of Life! Then we will be *one!*"

He suddenly paused, and I noted a tone of sorrow (perhaps horror) as He spoke again: "Tell them if they ignore or reject My love, if they turn away from My Father, if they refuse to listen to the urgings of the Spirit, there is nothing more that we can do for them. They remain under the control of Satan, that liar and deceiver, for whom I had to create hell when he defied the Almighty God. Because Jehovah is righteous, We had to punish Satan's wickedness and rebellion. I never intended a human soul to go to hell; in fact I came down from heaven and died for mankind to redeem him from that deceiver. I even went to hell and took the keys. I sealed Satan's fate, and secured victory over hell and death. Tell them, My name is above all names, but *they* must choose whom they will serve!"

Then His voice changed. Like a trumpet it echoed about the tomb: "*There is yet a little while—but very little!*"

I understood! I would scarcely have enough time, before His return, to go and tell them! I was being commanded to disclose whatever I would see that day. And beyond that message, my mind told me that He meant I would not die before His return—it would be that soon. He also meant that most of those in my audiences would not see death but would be caught up in the Rapture to meet Him! He is preparing to return for His earthly rule at Jerusalem, His headquarters. He as much as said, "I can't wait much longer; world events can no longer be postponed! These are the last days of which I spoke in the Upper Room."

The Pit of Hell

Suddenly, I was in hell! I knew I was trapped in the bowels of the earth. Instantly, I was in a stone, coffinlike cell, four feet wide and six and a half feet high. The terror was instantaneous and indescribable. With a sickening thud I felt my feet hit the rock floor. My lightning-fast mind added to the horror of this total isolation in stone by telling me all the answers to my sudden questions. Cast as an unsaved sinner, I was on death row in solitary confinement by my own choice. Satan had invited me, and I had not refused. I alone was to blame. I had died without accepting the love of Jesus about which I heard so many times. This is the pit of the first death, the holding tank of horror, Satan's stronghold for sinners.

I tried to scream—no voice. I pounded the walls and the ceiling—no escape. Total blackness. Total silence. Total stench. It had to be from demons. Sure enough. I looked down and saw clearly with the mind's eye of my fallen spirit-body many little, spiderlike demons about my feet. Among them were several deformed catlike and doglike creatures with black feces-matted fur. Despite their constant movement, each one fastened its gaze upon me as the smaller ones swarmed up the walls beside my face. Behind each eye were flames. The stench was nauseating.

My mind told me that they were the "chained demons" of Satan, and they agreed, saying, "We are the chained demons, here to haunt and taunt you in hell! And, Buddy, we'll do it!" (Their actual language was so foul, it cannot be repeated. The next day I asked Jesus to erase all memory of their demonic language, and He did.) "You could have accepted God as your Father and Jesus as Saviour. We read the Book. You're trapped with us now, and Buddy, we'll make this your hell. Aha. Aha. You fool!"

My Judge

In total despair I started to slide to the floor. Already there was no hope. But worse yet, I was suddenly snatched away and found myself standing before a gorgeous throne on which sat God, an indescribable personage. I knew Him by His radiance! He was rapidly thumbing through a large book in His right hand. I could see through its pages to the title on the cover: THE BOOK OF LIFE. I felt naked—physically, emotionally, spiritually. I knew I was being judged, and I had no lawyer to plead my case.

I found I had my voice again, and I heard it stammer: "What are You looking for, God? My name must be there!"

"I am looking for your name in our family album, but I do not find it here," He replied with a shake of His head.

"But it must be there, God! I lived a good life. I was never arrested or imprisoned. I obeyed the rules. I did good works. Look some more! What do You mean, I'm not in Your family?"

"You rejected My Son's offer to be born again, to be washed clean in His blood. Remember? You were told many times! There is nothing more I can do. You are not one of My children. You belong to Satan's family." He stretched forth His arm and pointed to a distant lake of fire.

I shall never forget what I saw: *the second death.* He explained, "It was prepared for Satan and his angels. Depart from Me into everlasting punishment with your father, the devil."

In a split second I was back in the pit, and I slid like ooze among the little demons on the floor. Then I was snatched upward and found myself standing in Lazarus's tomb with the light *on!* My two minutes in hell without Jesus had ended! The guard was shouting to the three of us to come forth.

"No, the fuse did not blow," he answered me. "Perhaps something else? Who knows? The light failed here." The children's voices filtered down: "Get your postcards here. Three fo' a dollah."

I remember nothing of the other events of that day. For months I could not overcome the horror of hell enough to report its terror without sobbing. The message of those two minutes was so clear: Jesus loves us so much that He voluntarily died to insulate us from Satan and save us from hell! On the other hand, Satan hates us so much he wants us in hell where he can destroy us.

We're Given the Choice

How can Jesus say it any more clearly than He did to me? "Tell them. Tell them. Tell them. They have a choice. There is yet a little time, but very little."

Jesus says, "Come forth. Shed your graveclothes. Join God's family." Jesus loves you, whatever your condition. He says, "Come as you are."

Jesus has made it utterly clear through His Word that God sees two kinds of people—rebellious souls and penitent souls. Rebellious souls are those who choose Satan. They work for him and are paid in "wages," redeemable in death at the time of their judgment. "And as it is appointed unto men once to die, but after this the judgment" (Hebrews 9:27). Penitent souls are those who choose Jesus, the Christ. They can work with Him and are given "gifts" redeemable in eternal life at the moment they are received. ". . . but the gift of God is eternal life through Jesus Christ our Lord" (Romans 6:23).

How exciting to know that *today* is the day the Lord has made for us to make our choice! We will rejoice and be glad therein if we choose Him.

Come, Let Us Reason Together

> Come now, and let us reason together, saith the
> Lord: though your sins be as scarlet, they shall be
> as white as snow; though they be red like crim-
> son, they shall be as wool.
>
> Isaiah 1:18

HAVE YOU EVER pondered what is God's wondrous invitation to man? Could it be the right to *reason* together?

A Parable

As a child did you ever lie awestruck in the fragrant
grass of a meadow sprinkled with baby-faced daisies and
fluttering butterflies and squint into the blue sky where
clouds changed shapes like magic to form misty animals
and towering castles? Did the wonder of it all capture
your imagination and call forth giggles of glee as though
you were free to float above the highest mountain? Without being told, you knew that Somebody Big was playing
up there!

Later as an "all wise" teenager you looked up again
(too busy to lie down this time), and you saw nothing but
wispy warnings that it might rain tomorrow and spoil

your skate-board contest. It was very hard to see anything but signs of weather. Dashing away in your hot rod you mentally noted that sun today and rain tomorrow would only make the weeds grow faster in the family garden and the lawn would require mowing sooner. Your weekend of escape was already ruined! "Can't anything go right for a change?" you grumbled.

Then that time did come when nothing went right. You simply seemed to lose control. When you had been in school, the teacher (and especially your parents) constantly "forgot" that you were a "grown person" who knew where it was really at! Now as a parent, you discover that there is no way to please the gang at home; you can't possibly meet their ballooning demands; and whatever you do for them is not appreciated anyway! "Best quit trying and call off the rat race!" you complain to yourself. "Life isn't worth it anymore." You wonder why you are forced to waste your life, now that you are grown up. Oh, well, hit the sack and forget it. . . .

That very night a still, small voice whispers through your tired brain, "Come." In curiosity you turn on your pillow and grunt "Yes?" It must be that nightcap talking back, you figure in disgust. Again it speaks, "Let us reason together." This sounds more logical than the mess you are in. "Why not?" you concede. "I've tried all the other tricks of the trade to make ends meet. Nothing works."

"Let us reason together, saith your Lord." It is louder this time! "What's going on? I am not dreaming," you convince yourself. But you did hear some kind of voice, twice now. "All right, whoever you are, let's reason!"

"Though your sins be as scarlet, they shall be as snow." This time the voice is loud. You wonder whose it is, and why so gentle.

"But wait a minute; what has *sin* got to do with my problem? You have the wrong fellow, Voice! Don't put that 'sin stuff' on me. I'm no devil; follow me around some day and watch how hard I work to do right by everyone. You won't see me getting into trouble with the law. After all, I live by the golden rule. You know I have never done anything wrong. Have I?"

Suddenly, as you await an answer, the movie screen of the mind lights up in the darkness of the night. You see yourself, as the head of the house at breakfast, screaming at your wife, Alice. There is a hateful look on your face. Your fists are clenched. Mike, Jr., peers at you over his bowl of cold cereal; he is taking a lesson in handling a "broad" in case he ever gets "stuck" with one when he grows up! The mental camera swings to pixie-faced Gloria, trying to shrivel herself up so she will fit under the edge of the table and can fly away to her imaginary world of joys and Barbie dolls.

Tears appear on Alice's blanched cheeks as she bolts through the bedroom door which she slams angrily behind her. Then they hear your VW's motor whine as you gun it into the street, headed for another day on that "goofed up" assembly line where you work.

The Intercessor

You are greeted by a cheerful voice: "You look like an escapee from a nightmare, old chum!" Sure enough, this

has to be Marv the Monk speaking. He had joined the
assembly-line crew six months back, when they needed a
real husky to swing the heavy rubber mallet that seats the
curved plate glass into the rear-window mountings. A
grunt would escape his throat whenever his huge brown
arms directed the single blow that forced a heavy glass
into the water-tight stops. He had earned his nickname
the very first day at work when the muffler man heard
him exclaim, "There's a blow for the Lord. Hallelujah!"
He *was* different. He *enjoyed* his job. He even smiled instead of smoking or cussin' during work breaks.

"You're looking the way I used to, Mike," Marv con-
tinues. "My wife and kids finally left me. Couldn't take
my crabbing and drinking! You know what I mean,
Mike?" For a big man, he has a soft voice.

"Okay, Marv, bug off. *My* problems are none of *your*
business. If I want help, I'll ask for it!"

"I sure hope you do! I once waited to ask for help till I
ended up falling off the curb one night, just a common
drunk! Next thing I knew a fellow was holding my head
up out of the mud. I reached up and felt a badge. He said,
'You can call me Larry. What's your name?' 'I'm Marv
Somethin', and I'm drunk.' 'Okay, Marv Somethin', you
need me, and I need you. Let's go talk it over.' Believe it
or not, that cop really talked like he was my brother!

"That cop told me Jesus loves drunks. I didn't know
anybody cared about me, much less God. He said that I
couldn't make it on my own. Things would only get
worse if I tried to drown them. He said all I needed was
Jesus, a real Friend who would save me from myself and

would carry all my burdens for me. He said God's Spirit could move right inside me and clean up sins and all.

"Okay, Mike, I'm about through, but here comes the miracle! That cop said, 'Man, tonight is your night to be set free! God wants your troubles solved without alcohol. You can say to Him: "Forgive me, Lord. I need you real bad. Take over and run my life." ' Well, Mike, I had nothing to lose, and I needed help right away. So I said that little prayer as best I could with my thick tongue. And I suddenly felt warm! Believe it or not, I was suddenly sober, and felt like I was clean inside. The cop said, 'Go home and find your wife and kids. Tell them Jesus loves the whole family. Next time I see you, you can ride with me and tell some other fellow in the gutter how to be set free!' Well, it's been a new life for me since then! I recommend it! I know I am reborn! That same prayer will work for you, Mike."

The Great Wonder Revealed

When God suspends operations in heaven in order to reason with one of us, it is truly a happening. To your natural mind, such a supernatural act may seem irrational and foolish. Perhaps you are telling yourself that the King of Kings might converse with a world potentate, but to take time out to talk with an ordinary person (taxpayer or inmate or hospital patient like you), well, that is too much. Nevertheless, He really is saying to you: "Come, let us reason together."

He wants to talk with you. There is no one else He

loves so much. God could have decided to talk to the animals or the trees or the earth, instead of talking to you. Therefore, if God is so preoccupied with getting *you* to come and reason (during this "enlightened" twentieth century), there must truly be a tremendous motive! What could it be?

The answer is simple: His children have troubles, bad troubles, and He has the answers, perfect answers. Their troubles are labeled *fear, despair, sin*. His answers are labeled *faith, hope,* and *love*. Their wages lead to *sorrow, pain* and *death*. His gifts lead to *joy, comfort* and *eternal life*.

The Almighty Creator spent ages seeking something more precious than His limitless universe. The Bible says that He fashioned a habitable globe, hung it in glittering space, and still could not rest. His eyes searched to and fro over the earth; something important was missing. In eagerness for an answer, He called a conference of the Trinity.

Amazed angels held their breath, galaxies spun attentively in the heavens; shimmering waters obediently caressed their limiting shores; and creeping creatures awaited in awe. At last a Voice shook the universe: "Let us make man in our image!" Then God smiled. He looked down and said, "It is very good!" He could rest.

Soon Jehovah looked around for His precious man. He had wandered away. So God went seeking again. When He finally found him hiding behind a tree, He said "Come, I love you." And man began to learn a truth: God needed someone to love! He still does—*it is you!*

And You Need Jesus

The omniscient God that made you has already done all the reasoning with His perfect mind. All He asks of you is to accept His anointed Son. How?

1. Swallow your pride (*see* Proverbs 16:18).
2. Open your heart (*see* Romans 10:10).
3. Accept God's gift of life (*see* John 10:28).
4. Confess Him as Saviour (*see* Romans 10:9).
5. Confess your sins daily (*see* 1 John 1:9).
6. Live victoriously (*see* 1 Corinthians 10:13).
7. Employ and enjoy prayer (*see* James 5:15, 16).
8. Serve your Lord daily (*see* John 12:26).

God says that this is the reasonable way to live. He knows! He is ready to reason *today!* Tomorrow may be too late.

He says, "Come, let us reason together."

Come, Thou and
All Thy House

And the Lord said unto Noah, Come thou and all
thy house into the ark; for thee have I seen righteous before me in this generation.

Genesis 7:1

WE HUMANS think we are in real trouble when one of us
has a nosebleed, or breaks a leg, or goes into labor, or
runs a high fever. The sirens whine, the emergency crew
grabs its equipment, and the sterile instruments are
quickly unwrapped! Even out-of-town relatives are noti-
fied to share the pathos!

God's Emergencies

When God declares an emergency, it truly exists! Since
no one else counts so much as does one of His children,
His solutions always involve their well-being.

If it weren't for His boundless love for each trouble-
maker, He could sit back now and enjoy His creation
from the absolute perfection of His throne. While sur-
rounded by His sensible and adoring angels, He could be
free to look out upon the endless expanse of His handi-

work, and become enveloped in His boundless joy. But God is not yet freed from overseeing His family!

Whenever His children create an emergency because of their faithlessness, He rolls up His sleeves to free His right hand for goodness and His left hand for mercy, and goes to work!

God's first emergency was *rebellion!* You will remember the record. It was on that fateful day when God's leading angel, Lucifer, the "bright star" and beautiful ruler of all other angels, shocked the heavenly hosts by striding up to God and announcing that he was taking over: "I will sit on your throne: I will be God!" (*see* Isaiah 14:13, 14).

And God said: "Out!" (*see* Isaiah 14:15). Jesus later recalled that He personally saw Satan fall to the earth from heaven as a bolt of lightning (*see* Luke 10:18). Emergency number one was thus handled in a split second. Satan had been dethroned forever.

God's second emergency was *deceit!* It occurred that fateful day when a second-rate, sneaky, slick Satan strode up to gullible Eve. He amazed her with his oily sales pitch which sounded exciting to her, more fun than God's strict "Creator's instructions." Satan declared that God had lied about the danger of eating anything from that certain fruit tree. "Anyone should know that its fruit is delicious and harmless! Certainly, you will not die if you eat the best fruit in Eden," he declared with mock authority. And Eve said, "Okay, boss, I'll try one piece" (*see* Genesis 3).

After she and Adam had eaten, they hid in shame.

Their innocence had suddenly fled. God came looking for them while they desperately donned fig leaves. "Where are you, Adam? I want you to come," He commanded.

In this greatest emergency, God knew that sin had entered the world through Satan's deceit.

He said, "Crawl on your belly. You are cursed!" He pointed to Adam and Eve and said, "Out," and they sneaked out of Eden, into a world of sweat and tears, pain and death.

Then Jehovah told Eve that the snake would bruise her seed's heel, but her seed (Jesus) will crush the snake's head and redeem all people. And the second emergency had been handled. God had made the plan of salvation and had defeated Satan, a born loser. Satan furiously fought back with every lie, hate, murder, perversion, atrocity, and disease that he could conceive.

On another day God's anger boiled when He found only one family in all the earth who still worshiped the Creator. All other peoples and their children were chasing after wickedness concocted by Satan, who now had power on earth. Wickedness thus became the third emergency.

God called Noah aside: "Build Me an ark! I am grieved in My heart at man's unrighteousness. I will wipe man off the face of the earth!" Genesis, chapters 6 and 7, will refresh your memory of this awful moment in history when man's ". . . every imagination of the thoughts of his heart was only evil continually" (Genesis 6:5). God thus removed the unbelieving nations with His flood of healing waters. The third emergency had been handled.

For proof of His sovereignty the Lord left several signs of the existence of the flood. Among them are: the geological evidences of a massive water-produced, mountain-moving, animal-destroying worldwide flood; pieces of an ark-sized boat on a mountainside of Ararat; and a rainbow set in the skies.

And Now

Do you remember what was said by Jesus Christ Himself, the Creator of the flood, when His disciples asked about the times of His return? Take careful note:

> But as the days of Noe were, so shall also the coming of the Son of man be. For as in the days that were before the flood they were eating and drinking, marrying and giving in marriage, until the day that Noe entered into the ark, and knew not until the flood came, and took them all away; so shall also the coming of the Son of man be.
>
> Matthew 24:37–39

Have you read your morning newspaper today? It could be reporting Noah's times! Item after item is a repetition of what he saw around him as he faithfully hammered on his ark:

- WARS ERUPT IN AFRICA, ASIA, CENTRAL AMERICA
- DIPLOMATIC MISSION FAILS TO PRODUCE ACCORD
- CRIME IN STREETS DESTROYS COMMUNITY LIFE
- TEENAGE ABORTIONS SKYROCKET UNDER HEALTH PLAN
- RAPES AND VENEREAL DISEASE REACH NEW HIGHS

- WORSHIP OF GOD UNDER SUPREME COURT ATTACK
- SANCTITY OF CHURCHES THREATENED IN COURTS
- GLUTTONY BECOMES A NATIONAL HEALTH CRISIS
- SUICIDES ESCALATE AS HOMELIFE DETERIORATES
- DIVORCES NOW PERMIT SEQUENTIAL POLYGAMY
- TEENAGE PROSTITUTION EMERGES AS BIG BUSINESS
- ABUSE OF PUBLIC FUNDS NO LONGER WORRIES COURTS
- RESPECT FOR NEIGHBORS REPLACED BY NUISANCE SUITS
- INTERNATIONAL ANGER GROWS DESPITE PEACE TALKS

Jesus said, "When you see these things, know that the end is at hand." Only His immense mercy for His children has stayed His wrath. He is giving them a few more days to find and accept Him as Saviour! "Watch therefore," He cautioned. "Blessed is that servant whom his lord when he cometh shall find so doing" (Matthew 24:42, 46).

Do you know that Jesus has prepared Himself as the modern-day Ark to rescue us for eternity? Not a temporary wooden boat this time, but an everlasting Rock of Ages to withstand the fires of eternal judgment to be meted out upon a sin-sick generation. God's mercy has secured our future.

Noah was wise: he listened to God, and was prepared for the flood. We can be wise too, by accepting His invitation: "Come thou and all thy house into the ark; for thee have I seen righteous." This word is for you. Exciting, isn't it?

Come Ye: Let Us Go Up Unto the Mountain

> And it shall come to pass in the last days, that the mountain of the Lord's house shall be established in the top of the mountains, and shall be exalted above the hills; and all nations shall flow unto it. And many people shall go and say, Come ye, and let us go up to the mountain of the Lord, to the house of the God of Jacob; and he will teach us of his ways, and we will walk in his paths: for out of Zion shall go forth the law, and the word of the Lord from Jerusalem.
>
> Isaiah 2:2, 3

REPEATEDLY THROUGHOUT Scripture, God is inviting you, and all His children, to come where He is, because He loves us! Since Jerusalem is His earthly home, He bids us to come to His mountain place. During His reign there, called the millennium, all nations will flow like rivers through the capital city of the earth in yearly pilgrimages (*see* Zechariah 14:16). What a glorious privilege for those who endure unto the end.

Already Jerusalem is tingling with excitement. Even before the tribulation and the subsequent millennium occur, we see the land of Israel virtually crying out in anticipation of the Messiah's soon arrival. The signs of Jesus' coming are appearing wherever believers or even mere students of prophecy look for the evidence. If you have not been there recently, let me share with you a few of the exciting observations we made.

Wonders seem to start when one sets foot in Israel. (*See* Isaiah 52:7.) On the TBN Holyland Tours, we wonder at first why we feel at home away from home. The soil under our feet seems to whisper, "Welcome home." Even the delays in customs, with the required inconveniences of baggage and passport inspection, seem not to dampen the tingle of anticipation at touching down on God's selected real estate!

A money changer illustrates the coming role of Jerusalem as the crossroads of commerce and international struggle for power.

Up the hills we travel, toward the Holy City, through new forests of "pine, fir, and box" just as predicted twenty-five centuries ago.

A look around the airport, along the highway, and into the marketplaces reveals this to be a crossroads of humanity with garbs of all nations, skins of all races, and life-styles spanning the centuries. We remember Isaiah's prophecy for this future day when, "Therefore thy gates shall be open continually; they shall not be shut day nor night; that men may bring unto thee [Jerusalem] the forces [wealth] of the Gentiles [nations] . . ." (Isaiah 60:11).

Prophecies Fulfilled

En route along the sloping foothills toward Jerusalem, we wind through man-made forests planted by Israelis and their friends from around the world. From the air we would see young woodlands springing up throughout the length of the country. In fact, we would be planting little trees there in a few days and saying a prayer of praise as we tamped the soil around the "new roots in Israel." Again we recall Isaiah's foretelling: "The glory of Lebanon shall come unto thee, the fir tree, the pine tree, and the box together, to beautify the place of my sanctuary; and I will make the place of my feet glorious" (Isaiah 60:13).

Around a corner and up a hill, we suddenly see the new Jerusalem of today spread across the hillsides. White at noon and pink at sunset, the stone block skyscrapers of modern Israel are a far cry from the shepherds' caves of Jesus' childhood. Behind us a high hilltop is crowned with a huge sprawling medical center, the pride of Israel's healers. Everything looks new and efficient as though typifying to the world what can result from the enthusiastic energy of a people driving ahead under self-controlled determination!

Was this what Zechariah saw? ". . . There shall yet old men and old women dwell in the streets of Jerusalem . . . . And the streets of the city shall be full of boys and girls playing. . . . I will bring them, and they shall dwell in the midst of Jerusalem . . . and I will be their God . . ." (Zechariah 8:4, 5, 8).

Prophecy is coming alive as the bus winds past bullet-scarred buildings where Israeli valor turned back bloody threats of defeat a few years ago. Isaiah foresaw 1948: ". . . His [the Lord's] hand is stretched out still. And he will lift up an ensign [flag of David] to the nations from far . . . and, behold. . . . None shall be weary nor stumble among them. . . . Their roaring shall be like a lion . . . yea, they shall roar, and lay hold of the prey . . ." (Isaiah 5:25–27, 29). We were seeing the visible proof of a reborn nation emerging as by a miracle through the rubble of centuries—because God had declared it!

Perhaps the most visible proof of this last-day fulfillment is a desert "blooming like a rose," as a prelude to the millennial promise of Isaiah 35:1 soon to be realized. ". . . for in the wilderness shall waters break out, and streams in the desert. And the parched ground shall become a pool, and the thirsty land springs of water . . ." (Isaiah 35:6, 7).

We learned that the vast amount of garbage and waste from the bursting cities is being hauled into the plains and wilderness. Wise agronomists have discovered that this refuse is ideal compost for the parched gravel and sand which is full of minerals. Once mixed, this renewed soil grows grain, vegetables, and fruits in unbelievable abundance—tons to the acre! For miles, we drove through this once-barren land, now laden with waving grains and oversized fruits and vegetables. North Africa, the Near East, and parts of Europe are already receiving the overflow of this gift of God to His returning people.

I was awed to see an oasislike area of greenery, as we drove toward Qumran along the Dead Sea road. I poked my guide: "Tell me, what keeps that large area at the

The cave of the Dead Sea Scrolls at Qumran is near the desert gorge where the present hatcheries are already prepared for the coming fish industry in the Dead Sea.

bottom of the valley over there so green?" "Underground springs," he replied. "Those are our many hatcheries full of fish. That is the valley which will split apart from Jerusalem to the Dead Sea when the Messiah touches foot on the Mount of Olives. The resulting huge river will wash the fish right into this sea to restore our fishing industry here. You must recall the prophecy?"

I did. Ezekiel long ago had quoted the Lord:

...These waters issue out toward the east country, and go down into the desert, and go into the sea: which being brought forth into the sea, the waters shall be healed .... and there shall be a very great multitude of fish, because these waters shall come thither ... And it shall come to pass, that the fishers shall stand upon it from Engedi even unto Eneglaim; they shall be a place to spread forth nets; their fish shall be according to their kinds, as the fish of the great sea, exceeding many.

Ezekiel 47:8–10

Reader, I ask you: How close must be the return of the Lord with the hatcheries awaiting the great river? It is exciting to read how Ezekiel (in the vision of chapter 47:1–7) waded out into the river three-and-a-half miles wide, from ankle deep to impassable. It won't be long until it flows!

Do you want another thrill? Follow us down many lad-

The day after the Egypt-Israeli peace pact, the Western Wall is already attracting Jew and Gentile worshipers who pray for the peace of Jerusalem and for the coming of the Messiah. Excavations at the site continue, far below the present ground level.

ders below the Western Wall until we stop at a recent
"deeper digging." Wooden shafts of a long ladder pro-
trude through a manhole in the dirt. Israel's leading ar-
cheologist points downward into the hole, explaining that
a few days ago, an exciting discovery stunned the work-
men: they uncovered an arch of hewn stone cemented
with glass-impregnated mortar.

"As Jehovah is my witness," he explained, "this must
be an entrance to the Holy of Holies. Our ancient docu-
ments state that Solomon used just such mortar here—no
place else." He mentioned that the university had certi-
fied the mortar as being of Solomon's era. A daily vigil is
now maintained at the site by Jewish priests, praying for
the safety of Jerusalem and for the coming of the Messiah
(*see* Psalms 122:6–9).

And that is not all we learned. They told us about the
fifty-or-so Levite priests being trained to perform animal
sacrifices upon their graduation in 1980. They described a
synagogue under construction, referred to as "The Temple." (Do you suppose the antichrist will use it as the center for his last-moment insults against God?)

Also of interest, in the summer of '79 I received word
from our Jerusalem-based missionary that she had just
returned from Samaria where she witnessed sacrifices of
scores of lambs performed by priests restoring their ancient rituals there.

Peace-pact Excitement

In the midst of our tour, the unexpected happened:
Egyptian President Anwar Sadat and Israeli Prime Minis-

ter Menachem Begin suddenly set a date to sign the pre-liminary peace pact! There we were in Jerusalem where the excitement exploded. The TV carried the picture from the White House, as crowds watched in wonder as prophecy became reality through the tube. As the ink dried and the participants hugged and President Carter smiled, the crowd came alive with shouts of joy and wonder.

In our hotel the band struck up the national anthems of Israel, Egypt, and the United States, with each assembled nationality joining in with those who knew the words. Momentarily, all celebrants became as one! Then the wine flowed, and the cake was cut. *Shalom* was here!

At the Wailing Wall all was in pandemonium. Locked-arm dancers of all ages hopped, jumped, or stumbled in

In a hotel lobby in Jerusalem, Israelis share the peace-pact ex-citement with tourists from America and the "uttermost parts of the earth."

the torch-lit rain and cold. Long-hushed songs of victory
and peace rang across the square. From hastily erected
platforms, politicians, rabbis, and song leaders yelled
their messages of *shalom* and joy. Cameras flashed while
our TV crew recorded the long-awaited fulfillment of
Israel's twenty-four-hundred-year-old prophecy. The
bearded priests recalled the memorized words of their
prophets; the young people were envisioning adolescence
without war!

Bible students know that God predicts sudden destruction in the end times when nations start to declare
"Peace, Peace," when there is no peace apart from the
Prince of Peace. We read in 1 Thessalonians 5:3: "For
when they shall say, Peace and safety; then sudden destruction cometh upon them. . . ."

However, in this prelude to the tribulation, we are seeing this very year the temporary lull in hatreds between
Israel and her neighbor, just as the Lord has planned in
preparation for the millennial peace. We read: "And the
Lord shall be known to Egypt, and the Egyptians shall
know the Lord in that day . . . . In that day shall there be a
highway out of Egypt to Assyria . . . . In that day shall Israel be the third [partner] with Egypt and with Assyria,
even a blessing in the midst of the land: Whom the Lord
of hosts shall bless, saying, Blessed be Egypt my people,
and Assyria the work of my hands, and Israel mine inher-
itance" (Isaiah 19:21, 23–25). P.S. The highway is under
construction now.

This is the home of Peter's mother, where Jesus stopped to heal her (foreground), and the synagogue (background) where Jesus delivered His message: "Repent, for the kingdom of heaven is at hand."

God's Special Favors

Your tour in Israel will provide another wonder! After all, God is primarily interested in people, hence He does special favors for His children while they are in His holy mountain. We saw some of them. As He promised so many times, He is faithful to perform. Miracles. Blessings. Liberations. Healings. Salvations. Jesus is still touching, touching, touching. Here are some examples.

In the Garden: I was on the outskirts of the crowd next to an olive tree as we stood in prayer. Suddenly, an elderly man slumped to the stony ground, as those next to him gasped in dismay—heart attack! Pushing my way through the people, I knelt to examine him. His heart had stopped, his pupils had dilated, his skin was already gray. Clinically, he was dead—a coronary. Praying hands were already laid on him. I added mine: "Now, Jesus, glorify Your Father with a resurrection. Thank You, Lord!" I opened my eyes and waited a moment. Suddenly his color returned, he gasped and tried to sit up. The miracle had happened. Throughout the rest of the tour, his eighty-year-old heart was perfect!

At the Upper Room: At the bottom of the narrow worn staircase, stood a sobbing young lady on one foot. "Doctor," she called to me, "I need a shot for pain. I can't go another step." Her hopes of worshiping in the Upper Room seemed shattered after the long trip from Los Angeles. "My foot was crushed under a truck two years ago. The bones are held together with a big nail, and the pain today is excruciating. Help me!"

I had nothing to offer but Jesus. I grasped her deformed foot, and spoke to my Healer: "You brought her this far, Jesus. Please get her up the stairs. We thank You."

Two hours later, still sobbing but now from joy, she ran to me over the broken gravel. "Look, look! When you prayed the pain instantly left. When I prayed in the Upper Room, I fell unconscious for fifteen minutes, and when I came to, I had a new foot. It's b—b—beautiful," she sobbed. I examined it—brand new, no nail, perfect functions. Jesus is a fast-working surgeon! We praised Him.

In the Upper Room, hands are raised in praise for God's out-pouring of love with "signs and wonders following."

Again, I heard my named being called. This time by the elderly lady who had been barely able to get around with her cane. She was pulling her two-piece cane apart as she walked toward me. "Here, keep it, Doc. I had two artificial hips put in me four years ago. When I finally made it to the Upper Room, I went to sleep on the floor, and when I awoke, I had new hips. Hallelujah, Jesus! Look, I can walk normally!" And she did. Jesus had said the stones could cry out in praise of Him. We know that bones can, too.

At the Pool: Satan once tried to defy God's holy mountain by tempting Jesus and then having Him crucified. In both attempts Satan failed to eliminate God. Ever since, he has been attacking God's children with bad habits which he labels "social graces."

North of the temple site, these excavated stones cry out: "Jesus walked here and dined with publicans and sinners in these ancient dwellings."

We saw inner healings. Standing under the lofty arches of the church building, we listened as the speaker asked the Holy Spirit to free anyone bound by bad habits. The Spirit searched hearts, and needy ones moved forward. Cigarette packs and lighters were thrown to the floor. Tears of joy welled as prayers for release from bitterness and unforgiveness were answered. Release from alcoholic bondage was declared. Personal family frictions faded. Several accepted Jesus as Lord for the first time. Satan again slunk away—defeated even by the prayers of the Nazarene's children. (He knows he's a born loser.)

On the Mount of Olives: God's Word has offered us authority (dominion) over the elements and over demonic

Jerry Barnard, Paul Crouch, Dr. Eby, Maybelle Eby, and Jan Crouch witness the fog's lifting. " 'Praise the Lord From Israel' is on the air, live from Jerusalem. Hello, California. On this very place—very soon—Jesus' feet will stand on the Mount of Olives!"

powers of the air or earth. We claimed it, and we saw the results. At 6:00 A.M. we were to be ready to send back TV signals by satellite to TBN's "dish" in California. We needed a miracle. The fog was too thick for the cameras to penetrate, and something was canceling the video signals to America. Satan was chuckling.

En masse our 250 partners agreed in prayer. In Jesus' name we rebuked the fog for obscuring our cameras, and we took authority over Satan who was interrupting the airways. The second hand ticked on while engineers on both sides of the world frantically tried to make contact. With seconds to go before air time, the fog dissolved as if by magic, and the sun's morning shaft hit the mount! The shouts of joy nearly drowned out the TV crew's simultaneous yells to Paul Crouch: "They've got us. It's loud and clear! Three, two, one, you're on." Browbeaten Satan had fled; he fears prayer.

The miracles went on and on. If only the nations, and especially God's individual children, would take Him at His word when He says: "Come to My mountain; come to Me for I alone am holy; let Me love away your cares and pains"; then heaven would be on earth already. Yes, He's coming anyway.

Are you watching?

Come Up Hither

After this I looked, and, behold, a door was opened in heaven: and the first voice which I heard was as it were of a trumpet talking with me; which said, Come up hither, and I will shew thee things which must be hereafter.

Revelation 4:1

HEAVEN IS SO exciting! Let me tell you something about it. But first, let's listen to what John has to tell us.

John's Visit to Heaven—A.D. 90

Jesus' beloved disciple heard a voice "like a trumpet." He tells us about this glory-filled vision in the Book of Revelation. After twenty centuries, it is still an unknown story to many persons. They are just now discovering that they are living when all prophecies are already or about to be fulfilled. It is exciting. John was so overcome that he fell on his face and wept with emotion at the wonders he was being shown. Carefully he described these awesome events in heaven and on earth when the King of Kings comes again to banish sin and exalt righteousness.

God invites you and me to share this blessing by simply reading or hearing about the words of that prophecy (*see* Revelation 1:3). In it Christ promises that He is returning soon and quickly to bless us in person (*see* Revelation 22:7). Even as you read and reread Revelation this week, God is on His throne, watching mankind polarizing into groups—the goats who elect to butt their way through life, and the sheep who choose to follow a wise Shepherd through their valley of shadows (*see* Matthew 25:31–33). Jesus leaves no doubt as to the destiny of these groups. It is either heaven or hell.

My Visit to Heaven—A.D. 1972

Jesus showed me my paradise in heaven five years before He showed me hell. I praise Him for His timing. Only after He showed me hell, did He commission me to go "tell them" about these proofs of His matchless justice and love which led Him to give His life for His children who wandered lost.

I must tell you about my experience in my paradise in 1972. Heaven is real. I saw some of it. Jesus has prepared a place in paradise for me, just as He promised in John 14:2, 3: ". . . I go to prepare a place for you. . . . that where I am, there ye may be also." I was instantly there after my head struck the concrete. A rotted railing had given away from a second-story balcony against which I had leaned to drop a heavy box to the ground. I had left the battered head and blood-drained body behind for a hospital crew to deliberate over whether to proceed with an autopsy. (The book *Caught Up Into Paradise* tells of these details.)

Obviously, Jesus had empowered my spirit, the real

me, to "come up hither." And there I was, with speed faster than light. Like Paul (*see* 2 Corinthians 12:2) and John (*see* Revelation 1:10), I experienced the indescribable amazement of being in and with God in a "prepared" paradise.

Jesus was not using my temporary visit to duplicate the experiences of those others to whom He had shown a glimpse of life after death. He was individually revealing to me how real His promises are and how great His love is. I was to be given personalized data for use in telling others that these are the last days before our Messiah returns for us and commissions us to reign as kings and priests as He promised two thousand years ago (*see* Revelation 1:6).

Because Jesus had said, "Come up," my spirit-body had instantly responded to the call of its Maker. I was there standing, not on a cloud, not on some artist's magic carpet, but upon solid ground. My feet had landed with a "thud," and with joyous excitement, I spontaneously blurted out, "Dick, you're dead!"

I noted an indescribably pervading sense of peace, joy, comfort, and release. I sensed eternal timelessness, coupled with a joyous ecstasy of feeling at home for the first time. Above all I could feel God in me—in fact, at the core of me. All these simultaneous sensations occurred so instantaneously that they were breathtaking, though I needed no breath.

I was feeling like a wandering pilgrim suddenly brought home—perhaps as a found child feels upon being restored to the blissful safety of his own bed after wandering lost and lonely. This aspect of heaven never occurred to me as being one of the greatest blessings of "being set free in Jesus," or as one of the major gifts of the eternal life. Only my Creator could fashion a home such as this glorious paradise I was enjoying in Him.

I had no memory of earth. Apparently, that is part of the privilege of being in heaven—the release from re-membering anything which was imperfect, unpleasant, or incomplete! Heaven contains no pain, no tears, no sor-row. All are earthly symptoms of the penalty of sin. No memory of a cursed earth remains in the renewed mind.

My New Mind

It was my *new mind* that instantly captured my admira-tion, wonder, and praise. Not at all like my earthly brain which works imperfectly and at a snail's pace in com-parison with this new mind in the spirit-body. But better yet, it was instantly apparent that I was thinking as though I had become part of God's mind. This was an ec-statically beautiful experience.

This liberated mind of the spirit-body was actually teaching me that the response to each thought would be a simultaneous answer or act. Before I could compose or complete a thought or wish, the answer was given or the requested action was occurring. The earthly brain and mind is, of course, in nowise similar to the mind I experi-enced in heaven (*see* Isaiah 55:8, 9). As I stood dumb-founded and stock-still, in awesome wonder over this glorious sense of freedom to think perfectly, I realized I was sharing the mind of Christ. It was like plugging into His mental circuit, in fact, like borrowing His omniscience to do my thinking. I was receiving His answers directly upon my mind with a speed of transmission which bypassed earthly speech and hearing.

I now realize that Jesus was showing me what Paul revealed in his first letter to the Corinthians, chapter 2: "We have the mind of Christ," and therefore, "we speak the wisdom of God in a mystery," because our faith does not "stand in the wisdom of men, but in the power of God" (*see* 1 Corinthians 2:16, 7, 5). This is how He reveals all things unto us by His Spirit.

Hallelujah! I was being shown a tiny bit of the fantastic truth of what it means to be made "a new creature in Jesus Christ." By simply telling Jesus that we accept His loving purposes for our lives, He presents us to His Father as a "son of God," a King's kid, with a newly inherited right to think as He does (*see* 2 Corinthians 5:17; John 1:12).

Never on earth had I felt this total ecstasy of being one with God. As I stood there, I realized that God was with me, in me, surrounding me. I did not see Him visibly as I looked around paradise; in fact, it seemed totally unnecessary. In this place He had made for me, I was totally enveloped in His presence. No way can a human brain on earth completely comprehend this state of "oneness"with the Godhead because of our incomplete surrender of our self-consciousness and all of its prideful shortcomings.

I was being shown what Jesus really meant when He

prayed to the Father in John 17:21–23, 26, asking, "That they all may be one; as thou, Father, art *in* me, and I *in* thee, that they also may be one *in* us: that the world may believe that thou hast sent me. And the glory which thou gavest me I have given them; that they may be one, even as we are one: I *in* them, and thou *in* me, that they may be made perfect *in* one . . . . that the love wherewith thou hast loved me may be in them, and I *in* them." In paradise I was suddenly enjoying the fulfillment of Jesus' prayer—somehow by His miracle of grace, I was "in Him."

My New Body

After absorbing this dose of ecstasy, I reacted like a child with a new toy. I wanted to try out this new body in its beautiful environment. Truly, I felt like a child— peaceful, innocent, unburdened, unpressured, unfettered, curious, enthusiastic, secure, and totally consumed with love. I could feel the timelessness of eternity like a sixth sense. No sense of hurry, hurry—I could stand, look, listen, and enjoy forever. I was totally excited with the overwhelming joy, comfort, and peace which pervaded me and the created beauty of this place. A sense of total freedom overwhelmed me beyond description.

I looked down to see what it was my feet had so solidly contacted with a "thud" upon my arrival. It was firm ground, a planetlike creation. Green grasses grew thickly and without a single broken blade. Each growing thing was emitting its own light in whatever color was appropriate. White flowers thickly carpeted the huge valley floor, and I gasped upon noting that each was seemingly lighted from within with a whiteness I had never seen on earth. I asked the question of God: "How can these flowers be so exquisitely white?"

Instantly, came the answer: "Son, on earth you saw only the *reflected* light from the s-u-n, here we have the *perfect* light from the S-O-N who is the light of heaven. In Me all things exist and have their being."

In surprise I saw flowers within my legs, up to my knees. I decided to lift one leg free from the flowers in case I had bruised one of these gorgeous, self-illuminated, pure white, perfect, four-petaled lilies of the field. That was when I discovered how my new mind worked. My foot was already off the flowers before I finished deciding to lift it! The flowers never wiggled, so I put my foot back down. They reentered within my legs—motionless, unbruised, perfect. They didn't know they were being stepped upon. I was being told that this new body was like the one that Jesus had possessed as He rose through the graveclothes and walked out through the sealed stone door of the tomb, without touching either. He had left the wrappings like an intact, emptied cocoon for Peter and John to witness in amazement after daybreak that Sunday morning. As Paul had reported already, I was "bearing the image of the heavenly" (*see* 1 Corinthians 15:49).

In childlike glee I decided to try out my body by walking through the grasses, the flowers, and finally a tree. They ignored my intrusion. They must have grown used

to such experiments. The material of my body was unknown to me—cloudlike, gorgeously self-illuminated,
and transparent to the direct gaze—no bones, organs, or
blood (*see* 1 Corinthians 15:50). It was the identical size
and shape of my old earthly body, but unscarred and totally comfortable. It instantly responded to any thought I
gave it. Jesus had prepared for me a perfectly made-
whole, totally healed body, which was at peace with me
and my Maker.

As a physician, I was astounded upon examining myself to find this new body so exquisitely different. Yet it
was *me*. I was the same person here, just as before, on
earth, I had already by faith accepted as fact that the "real
me" must be a spirit who resided in the physical body
which I could see and feel. But that body was reluctant to
stay well or to perform adequately the tasks and skills
which I expected of it. People had identified that body as
"me," seldom if ever noting the real boy or man inside
it. Even I, on earth, had often been more concerned with
the container than with the contents!

Now I was seeing me—without that body of tissues,
cells, muscles, bones, brain, or whatever! Instinctively, I
knew that this celestial body could not die. I blurted a
question: "Lord Jesus, why is there no death in heaven?"
Again an instant answer: "Only organs can die! The spirit
is eternal. We made it in Our image."

I looked at me again. What a beautiful, homogeneous,
perfect, self-illuminated, cloudlike, weightless body! I
was wearing a single brightly lit pure white robe of rare,
rare fabric. I felt it—silklike yet firm. The Bible says it is

the linen of heaven, to be worn by saints (*see* Revelation 19:8).

Then I noticed I was neuter, sexless. Quickly, I asked, "Why am I neuter?" Instantly came the answer: "I never told mankind to repopulate heaven—only earth. Up here there is no marriage. Everyone here is created or reborn." I immediately felt foolish for having asked such a needless question (*see* Matthew 22:30; Genesis 1:28).

My Paradise Valley

I looked away from the remarkable body that I had just examined. I saw my paradise valley. With the eyes of the spirit-body, I could see like an eagle—ten miles seemed like ten inches—and without glasses. The scene was gorgeously unsurpassable in its beauty. Its foliage had a radiance. Not a shadow anywhere. In joy I waved my arms back and forth to test for shadows. Sure enough, heaven had no shadows. Just as He promised me in John 14:2, ". . . I go to prepare a place for you," He had made my paradise a valley of the things He knew I would enjoy—a great outdoors of mountains, trees, flowers, music, and sweet smells. Everywhere I sensed His presence, which is love, the *agape* kind.

For miles it seemed, there stretched rolling hills under cloudless skies of a color new to me, of an iridescent white-gold light. Flawless evergreens covered the hills which rose from the flower-carpeted valley floor. The trees somewhat resembled arborvitae but were too stately and perfect to be earthly. I saw no trees that appeared to be deciduous. Every leaf and branch was perfect and similar. I asked a question: "Why do the trees and flowers appear identical to each other?" The immediate answer: "In heaven creation has remained perfect. Where perfection exists, things grow alike."

Beds of gorgeous, white, four-petaled flowers amazed me. Instinctively, I decided to pick a bouquet for Maybelle and found the flowers already in my hand! The stamens, pistils, and calyxes of each flower were of liquid gold. I could see lengthwise through them to the stem. Now I know that "liquid gold" is not a poetical myth—it's a heavenly truth! Even more surprising was the feel of the stems—no moisture. Yet they were vibrantly alive and perfectly formed. They felt like dry velvet, soft as silk. I gasped in wonder: "Why no moisture; how can they live?"

I heard Him reply: "Son, on earth you had a temporary life support called H-two-O. In heaven we need no oxygen or hydrogen. Here we have the Living Water that flows from the throne of God." I should have known the answer before asking: He had given it to the woman at the well two thousand years ago. " . . . thou wouldest have asked of him, and he would have given thee living water" (John 4:10). It was supremely exciting to know that I was holding flowers, the very stems of which were being vitalized by the Living Water, one of the many manifestations of the Spirit of God. Jesus knows that even these lilies of the field have a message for us. He told the disciples to learn from them how not to worry (*see* Matthew 6:28).

Music of Heaven

All this time I had been aware of heavenly "background music" which seemed to fit unobtrusively into the total scene. Now I listened closely. It was beautifully different from anything on earth. In a twinkling I discovered why: it had no beat, and it came from everywhere! I also noted that my white gown, besides emitting a pure white light, was singing softly—as was my body, the flowers, trees, hills and sky (*see* 1 Chronicles 16:31–33). I started to ask God, "Why no beat?" but I already had the answer: "This is eternity where timelessness cannot be divided up into beats." It was that simple! Then I asked God from where was the music coming.

"Do you not remember your law of physics, son?" I heard Him ask. I knew He meant the law of resonance, whereby two objects of similar material, density, and tension vibrate in unison when one is activated. "*I* created heaven and everything in it. It vibrates with me. *I* am the Composer. *I* have given heaven this new song." "Of course," I murmured, "only Jesus can compose such music as I am hearing." (In Revelation, John reports a "new song" in chapter 14, verse 3; I was hearing a preview.) The music was flowing from the throne!

Heavenly Perfume

A delicate aroma had been pervading my paradise. I stopped to enjoy it, and closed my eyes in delight. Such exquisite fragrance had to be limited to heaven, I realized, since it was fit only for the King. I asked Jesus for the explanation: "Where does it come from?" No answer! The following day in my hospital room I again requested an explanation, and I heard Him say, "Search the Scriptures, son. In them you will find the truth."

The truth was that I had been bathed in that special heavenly perfume described from Genesis to Revelation as "sweet-smelling savors." I had been given a preview of God's fantastic chemistry whereby He converts the ill-smelling smoke of Old Testament sacrifices, and the poorly worded prayers of the New Testament saints into an aromatic perfection fit for the King of Kings (*see* Leviticus 1:9). Because these forms of worship represent obedience to God's Word, He has saved every atom of the distilled elegance in golden vials to be opened that great day when we shall all praise Him before the throne (*see* Revelation 5:8; 8:3, 4).

What a privilege to know that our prayers are of such eternal pleasure to our loving God. What great value He places upon us. He even allows us to smell like a sweet savor when we have been obedient (*see* 2 Corinthians 2:15–17).

The Straight and Narrow

So far I had seen no one else in my paradise. Jesus had been busy transmitting thoughts between our minds. I was being told how much there would be to learn about reigning with God throughout eternity. Nothing in my earthly schooling could prepare me for His heavenly program.

It seemed that we had been "talking" mind to mind for a long time, although there is no time in heaven. I eagerly wanted Maybelle to share with me these indescribable joys. Since we had been "one flesh" on earth (*see* Genesis 2:24), I expected to find her in a paradise, somewhere nearby. Not knowing what event had released me from earth to go to heaven, I was sure she, too, must have had the same "ascension." So I thought, "I will go looking for her down this valley." Instantly, I found myself walking, or floating, effortlessly, one foot in front of the other down a perfectly straight path which had appeared through the vegetation of the valley floor. It was the width of my foot—neither a flower nor a grass blade was being touched as I walked, nor did my feet quite touch the ground.

At that moment it seemed entirely normal that there should be a path. Only now do I wonder what it was meant to tell me. Straight and narrow? (*See* Matthew 7:14.) A heavenly way of walking? Yes. (*See* Psalms 16:11.) Proof that a child of God can walk unswervingly? Probably. (*See* Proverbs 4:11.) I gave it no thought; I was seeking Maybelle, too excited to analyze a path. I held my bouquet delicately, glowing like a torch in front of me (*see* Proverbs 4:18). Then I heard her voice.

From around a curve in the valley floor, she was calling, "Richard, Richard." I found my body rushing toward the voice. Then all went black and blank. Jesus had put my spirit-body back into that mud-body with its stitched scalp and tortured tissues. He had honored those intercessory prayers of Maybelle's many friends who had asked Jesus for a Lazarus-like miracle. Incidentally, He has handfuls of other miracles He wants to give, if His people will ask (*see* Matthew 7:7).

My paradise experience had come to an end. Jesus had shown me the realities of His promises. He had shown me that things unseen by our limited optic nerves are truly eternal; that the presence, the power, and the plans of the Saviour exceed our present imagination; that only by faith in Him, through His love for us, can He share the fantastic realities of the "prepared place" which He has set aside for His children! He long ago told us the same truths in 1 Corinthians 2:9, 10. Now He is telling us again in this last generation of the seventies and eighties to become His children, before it is too late. He already has His "marriage table" set and readied on high for you and me. If we simply answer His RSVP to come up hither, what banquet joys there will be with Jesus as host (*see* Revelation 19:9).

Although I was suddenly back on earth and unconscious, Jesus was not through with my lesson on miracles and wonders. I was to discover more of His compassionate love in a few hours when He would awaken me in an intensive care unit to tell me more. I could never forget that He had given me the proof that what I was to "tell them" was real, that their loved ones who had died in the arms of Jesus are in His presence filled with ecstatic joy, that He is awaiting the moment when He can have every child of His family with Him eternally.

I had "come up hither" and had seen His glory. "And

the glory which thou gavest me I have given them . . ."
(John 17:22).

Now a wonder-filled day in the hospital awaited me.

I Will Heal Him

For thus saith the high and lofty One that inhabiteth eternity, whose name is Holy; I dwell in the high and holy place, with him also that is of a contrite and humble spirit, to revive the spirit of the humble, and to revive the heart of the contrite ones . . . . I have seen his ways, and will heal him: I will lead him also, and restore comforts unto him and to his mourners. I create the fruit of the lips; Peace, peace to him that is far off, and to him that is near, saith the Lord; and I will heal him.

Isaiah 57:15, 18, 19

TO MY AMAZEMENT when the blackness of unconsciousness blew away like a fleeing cloud, my lids fluttered open to reveal an ICU hospital room, badly blurred. I tried to move to relieve the agony in every cell. I was paralyzed.

Above me hovered a hazy form in black attire with a Roman collar. "It" seemed to be sprinkling something over my body. I heard myself ask, "Are you a chaplain?" The faint answer came back, "Yes, I am giving you the rites of the church." I assumed he didn't wish to say "last rites."

"But I am going to live, Father," I murmured as he turned to leave. "You see, I just came back from heaven!" He turned back and bent low over my face where I could see his ashen look as though in shock. Then he bolted for the door with a parting promise: "I'll light another candle." He would return during the following two days to talk with the "dead man." A dear soul was he, reviving daily from this unexpected contact with a miracle.

The Cloud

In paradise, Jesus had not appeared to me in a visible form, because He had other plans. It was His intent to make a "hospital visit." He would come to heal.

He waited until I came out of the unconscious fog to find myself in a darkened room. Obviously, this was the night shift. A shadowy form sat at my side. "You are a nurse?" I murmured. "Yes, and I'll be with you till you die. Don't worry," a voice reassured me.

This was my opening: "But I won't die; you see I have just been sent back from heaven!"

"Think what you want," the voice replied, "after all, there is no God."

I sensed a challenge; perhaps I was sent back here to talk to her about the existence of Jesus. Witnessing to her would also take my mind off of the agony exploding in every tissue of my paralyzed body. How long I talked with her about God and heaven, I do not know, but suddenly I noted a brilliance throughout the room, although only a night-light was feebly glowing near the baseboard.

"This must be a miracle," I told myself. And there it

was—a brilliant pure white object emerging through the glowing plaster at the corner of the room next to the ceiling. I was transfixed with wonder as I watched it detach from the plaster and float over to me. I wanted to sit up and touch it—oh, just to be able to feel those exquisitely sculptured billows too beautiful to describe!

Intellectually, I knew what "it" must be: the same *Shechinah glory* that settled upon the Ark of the Covenant; the cloud that led the children of Israel through the wilderness by day, the cloud that Jehovah had used to enshroud Himself on the many occasions when He wished to talk to humans without blinding or blasting them with the power of His presence. I realized that He had come to my room to talk to me. I was overwhelmed with this new evidence of His love. And then the Cloud spoke.

"My son." With that salutation, He instantly exalted me and humbled me. What a voice! None other under heaven is like it—regal, sovereign, authoritative, loving, compassionate, meek, powerful. Anyone hearing that voice would know that the speaker is the Word of God, the Word from God, with God, the very God.

He continued, "My peace I give unto you." It seemed ridiculous for Him to talk of peace when I was in physical agony.

"With your hands you will heal." Again it seemed unbelievable that Jesus was ignoring my bloodless, paralyzed, useless hands. Bewildered, I suddenly discovered that I could hear and see perfectly now in His presence, yet I reflexly blurted out my human reaction.

"You must be kidding!" Instantly, I was ashamed, but I

couldn't retract those faithless words. Inwardly, I shuddered, "What will He do to me now?" The Cloud never moved. It just hung there another moment, and from it I heard again, "My peace I *give* unto you." Suddenly, the pain began receding from my fingers and feet, up the arms and legs, and disappeared as though being vacuumed from my motionless body. Again, came the Voice: "With your hands you will heal." With this promise, the Cloud receded to the corner of the room and slowly disappeared through the wall. The room went dark.

I realized that in His presence, my body felt healed! My five senses had been made perfectly normal. My mind had been momentarily like His, like "yesterday's" mind in heaven! I realized He had actually told me that I would live, would return to practicing medical skills, and would receive the gift of healing.

He would use *my* hands as *His*, with a touch of divine power, when my human hands were not in themselves strong enough to cast out diseases or devils. Then I fell asleep, without human sedation.

Truths He Showed Me

The Lord let me season steadily while He repaired tissue after tissue. Spiritually, He gave me time to absorb and digest and exult over the new dimensions of His love and power which I now better understood.

Day by day He provided the strength I needed for *that day.* Faithfully, He helped us meet our bills and pledges until I could return to the pressures of practice. He was showing me certain truths, which I wish to share with you. I will pick out a few of the important ones.

Truth One: Do not rely upon what you see. Rely upon the Almighty God! Use what you see or sense only as a basis or background for your prayers and praise to Him. Since you cannot see tissues healing or chemistry changing, rely instead upon Jesus' eyesight and promises to direct your healing. How could you know when a broken bone or heart is healed? Who can really heal anything except your Healer? All He asks is your faith that He is able (*see* John 14:13–15) and your confidence that He is working on your need.

Truth Two: Keep on praising the Lord for His promises. Once you ask Him to assume charge of your problem, do not walk away and forget Him. Instead, forget the problem and praise Him for faithfulness. Since you cannot solve your own spiritual problems by yourself, don't interfere while He is working on the details. Don't nag; don't fuss. He has promised to supply your needs if you get out of the way and let Him work with you. Keep on thanking Him for the answer that you know is on the way; then He can bestow it twice as fast.

Truth Three: Exercise your spirit of forgiveness. When the Lord's answer seems unduly delayed, it is your fault, not His. He told us where the trouble lies, just as He told his disciples one day. Let's read His words: "Therefore I say unto you, What things soever ye desire, when ye pray, believe that ye receive them, and ye shall have them. And when ye stand praying, *forgive*, if ye have ought against any [one]: that your Father also which is in heaven may forgive you your trespasses. *But if ye do not forgive, neither will your Father which is in heaven forgive* . . ." (Mark 11:24–26, *italics added*).

In other words, your Father had to forgive you for everything just to save you by grace. Now, you must be willing to forgive other humans in order to be eligible for God's gifts. Simple, isn't it? Just obey Him.

Truth Four: Confess Jesus before others. It should be obvious that Jesus will heal and bless you for one glorious purpose—to make you more effective as His ambassador of the Good News. He is literally advertising for more workers in His ripening fields (*see* Matthew 9:37, 38). To work with God, you must first confess Him and then be "in Him." John tells us: "Whosoever shall confess that Jesus is the Son of God, God dwelleth in him, and he in God" (1 John 4:15). Try God's way—there's nothing nearly so exciting!

How These Truths Work

Let me illustrate these truths with four simple examples that we have seen in our lay ministry this year.

Truth One: Do not rely upon what you see. A scrawny-looking thirteen-year-old Mexican boy leaned weakly upon his tearful mother's shoulder. She asked for prayer that he would survive tomorrow's open-heart surgery intended to repair a "hopeless congenital heart defect." "Why not ask for a new heart?" I queried. "God is such a good cardiologist!" The boy looked puzzled, and I asked him if he knew that Jesus can heal hearts. His mother answered for him: "That would be wonderful."

"In Jesus' name, heart be healed," I prayed and touched his forehead. We could see no change that morning. However, twenty-four hours later after repeated EKGs, the amazed surgeons at the university center declared his heart "normal" and sent him home unoperated. Only Jesus knows where that healthy heart came from, or how He put it into that chest!

Truth Two: Keep on praising the Lord for His promises. This woman from Hollywood was bothered by hurting joints. "Two years ago they were healed by prayer," she complained, "but it didn't last. God doesn't love me anymore."

"Who do you think is to blame, you or Him?" I asked.

"Well—He didn't keep His promise, it looks like," she fretted.

"Will you promise to praise Him right now and daily in return for another healing? *He* never quit loving you, but you got in His way," I informed her. Her face beamed with sudden understanding.

I touched her forehead and prayed: "Through the power of Jesus, be made whole." The Spirit dropped her to the floor, her hands went skyward, and I heard a strange language from her lips. Five minutes later, she stood up praising her Lord for her normal joints. Obviously, He and she had been in conversation about *her* faulty faith, and now there was nothing between them.

Truth Three: Exercise your spirit of forgiveness. In a Full Gospel Business Men's Fellowship International healing service last fall, we met a sorrowful lady, with tears of inward pain dripping from her cheeks. "You need help from Jesus, don't you," I whispered to prevent the surrounding crowd from eavesdropping on her problem. "Yes. My husband filed for a divorce today, after months of our fighting at home. I've prayed that our home wouldn't be broken, but I can't help hating him for the way he acts," she sobbed.

I could feel the spirit of bitterness like a fog exuding through her skin. She had been emotionally bound as if by chains, and she couldn't break free by herself. The Holy Spirit whispered to me, "I will bind that demon, and I will set her free." "God has already answered you," I told her. "In the name of Jesus, you are set free. Your marriage is preserved this day." She fell forward with such force that we both crashed to the cement floor. My glasses were flung across the room and broken.

In the last burst of frustrated anger, the defeated demon took off. I looked at her lying there, talking with her Lord—a smile on her face, and a glow about her wet cheeks. She had been set free! As she got up, I heard her exclaim: "I'm not bitter any more. I feel all the burden has gone. I can love him! Jesus, I love You so . . . ," and her voice trailed off as she headed for home and husband.

Truth Four: Confess Jesus before others. There are so
many examples, but I'll choose one—an eleventh-hour
miracle. The "Spirit Song" and our "team" had said the
benediction in a crowded college auditorium. We invited
folks to stay on for a healing touch from Jesus. *Was everyone sick?* I thought as they were all coming forward! At the
front of the line stood a shaky, skinny, sickly looking
twenty-three-year-old woman. She looked desperate. "I
must be healed tonight," she blurted. "If not, I will com-
mit suicide before midnight. My pistol is loaded at
home."

I took her pale face in my hands: "Jesus loves you,
honey. Don't disappoint Him by being foolish. Do you
know Jesus in your heart?" "Oh, yes, but I was born
without a third lumbar vertebra, and I can no longer
stand the pain. One leg is partly paralyzed and two
inches shorter than the other. All my life I have worn
braces or casts, but they didn't help. I've worn out all
known sedatives; even a shot of morphine every hour
does no good anymore. I can't believe God wants me to
suffer. I can't take it any longer. Please pray for my healing tonight. Please?"

As she spoke, I was noting the short leg, the curvature,
and the indentation from the missing vertebra. She was
already skin and bones from years of pain and drugs.

"Will you tell others about your miracle when Jesus
heals you?" I asked.

"Oh, yes. I know Jesus *can* heal me."

"All right, honey, you and He start talking about a
miracle. Ask Him for a huge dose of faith right now!"

I felt a sudden warmth radiate from her head and back as I asked for a creative miracle in her body. Her eyes closed. Jesus seemed to be holding her erect. I stood back in amazed joy, then turned to pray for two diabetic victims, while Jesus was healing the girl. Five minutes later she "awoke" with sobs of joy. "I am healed!" she shouted. "There is no pain anywhere! Look. My legs are the same length. My back is straight. Jesus healed me. Look, people, at what He did!"

Her joy was contagious. I bent over to examine her lower spine—there were five bony segments where I had counted four just minutes ago! Her hips were level; her spine straight. She could touch her toes for the first time in her life. She did every lumbar exercise I could think of. She could have passed any physical exam. God had put back a vertebra and hooked it up with all the complex attachments. The audience was applauding in amazement. Today, Jesus has a healthy young lady witnessing to His almighty power.

Lest We Forget Who Does the Healing

I am learning the secret to the joy which born-again Christians experience and radiate: it is *power. This power can be yours.* Jesus is not kidding when He asks you to believe that He loves you and has *all power (see* Matthew 28:18). He wants to make this power His gift to you if you will let Him enter and run your daily life by faith. The joy comes from putting the power to work.

Jesus is the expert Healer. He alone can instantly or

gradually cure, heal, or replace tissues in the mud-body
that He created and made alive. He also knows about
man's abysmal frailty, namely the ease with which his
memory can forget a previous healing. Almost before
some miracles can be fully enjoyed, the recipients are off
on another quest for something else from the Lord.

Mankind has the gimmees, and gimmees do not build
faith. Jesus knows this. Therefore, more often than not,
He must dole out His blessings a measure at a time, so
His children will learn that they must thank Him for each
comfort and healing. During this time, He is wisely test-
ing and strengthening their faith in order to develop their
"spiritual muscles" for a larger blessing. Impatient believers get cranky when they fail to see results right now.
Others wisely pray first for wisdom, and then for healing.
They find in any supposed delay a time to praise the Lord
for all His other promises.

King David realized that man was guilty of forgetfulness. To himself and to you he wrote: "Bless the Lord, O
my soul, and *forget not all his benefits:* Who forgiveth all
thine iniquities; who healeth all thy diseases; Who re-
deemeth thy life from destruction; who crowneth thee
with lovingkindness . . . so that thy youth is renewed like
the eagle's. The Lord executeth righteousness and judgment for all that are oppressed" (Psalms 103:2–6 *italics
added*). David said, "Forget not."

Let Them Have Dominion

And God said, Let us make man in our image, after our likeness: and let them have dominion over the fish of the sea, and over the fowl of the air, and over the cattle, and over the earth, and over every creeping thing that creepeth upon the earth.

Genesis 1:26

Thou madest him to have dominion over the works of thy hands; thou hast put all things under his feet.

Psalms 8:6

And hath put all things under his feet, and gave him to be the head over all things to the church, Which is his body, the fulness of him that filleth all in all.

Ephesians 1:22, 23

ONE OF THE BEST-KEPT secrets about God's love for His children has been His available gift of dominion. It may still be a secret to many even though Moses wrote about it quite a while ago.

Simply stated, the truth is this: *dominion*—mastery, authority—over things on the earth was transferred to man from the Creator—Jesus—the day He arrived in Eden.

Along came Satan and bribed man out of his rightful dominion. Then came the Creator, offering to give it back to man if:

1. He would repent of having submitted to Satan's offer of false power
2. He would believe in Jesus as the Way, the Truth, and the Life
3. He would willingly receive this power through the baptism of the Holy Spirit (*see* Acts 1:8), and would go and do something about it.

The secret is now out! Every believer who is willing to surrender his will, energies, and time, has Jesus' gift of unlimited power to exercise dominion—even over our enemy Satan! Have you read Jesus' own words?

> Behold, I give unto you power to tread on serpents and scorpions [demons] and over all the power of the enemy [Satan]: and nothing shall by any means hurt you.
>
> Luke 10:19

Translating this into modern terms, it means if you, as a disciple, have accepted this power over the very rulers of the principalities of the air (demon legions around the earth), then you also have dominion over lesser things around you.

Present-day Examples

Guatemala City was the setting for some great evidences of this dominion last year. Our group of fifty TV partners arrived in the previously earthquake-shattered city eager to share with the Mayan descendants whatever the Spirit had for their ears and hearts. Satan was angry and had ordered his "lieutenants" to dish out trouble, canceling everything for the day.

I was handed a note at the hotel registration desk, telling me that Manuel Bonillas, our TV evangelist and advance man in Guatemala, was at that very moment leaving for an emergency meeting with a score of local pastors. At 10:00 P.M. the night before, he was informed that they were canceling the huge crusade which they had previously agreed to sponsor this week. Reason? "There must be some sinister motive for fifty Americans to come here for *free*. We fear that they will disrupt the work of our local churches."

Manuel had written: "Pray immediately. Bind Satan. Release the Holy Spirit to free these people."

Our group moved into an adjoining room, while curious employees stared at us, we prayed: "Dear Lord, bind Satan and loose the pastors' hearts. Holy Spirit, we ask You to bestow a spirit of forgetfulness upon their minds to blot out the thoughts that Satan has placed in them. Praise the Lord! We accept Your answer."

At 4:00 P.M. we met a victorious Manuel in the lobby. *"Sēnores,* it was be-yoo-tee-ful! They cooed nawt remember thah rees-on for calling that mee-ting! They are so ex-ci-ted you came! *Gloria a Dios!"* He hugged all of us.

Storm, Go Away

Our next attack involved the weather. The eighty-seven-thousand-seat stadium echoed with the shouts and

claps of welcome from sixty thousand throats of weary
families who had trudged for days and miles under a hot
sun. They wanted to hear about the Americans' God of
love, and they were excited to have gotten seats. They
heard the Latin evangelist exclaim:

> Porque de tal manera amo Dios al mundo, que Dio a su
> Hijo unigenito, para que todo aquel que cree en el, no
> perezca, mas tenga vida eterna.
>
> Juan 3:16

And they answered with a roar of *"Gloria!"*

The echo had hardly died down when the sun dimmed.
A huge black storm front raced from the ocean toward
the stadium, obscuring the adjacent suburbs in a cloud-
burst. A spirit of fright gripped the standful of spectators:
they remembered a similar storm just before the great
earthquake that had leveled the city only a few months
ago! Children started crying, pulling parents toward the
exits.

We were about to see a miracle. "In the name of Jesus,"
shouted the evangelist, "we take authority over you,
storm! You are to stop where you are and leave us alone.
We are God's children, here to worship Him. Now, go
away, in the name of God Almighty!"

The crowd became silent. They were watching that
mighty storm front roll back as if in fear of approaching
the stadium. Our cameras turned upward to film the
hand of God at work. A stadium-sized hole was being
punched through that churning cloud. The ninety-degree
sun poured down on us inside the stadium walls, while

It rained all around us, but we stood on dry ground as the sun shone and we prepared to share with thousands of Guatemalans the miracles He had in store.

those outside ran for cover. Not a drop fell on the amazed crowd. The sermon started on time.

In conclusion, we heard the preacher say:

> Venid a mi todos los que estais cansados y agobiados, y yo os dare descanso.
>
> Mateo 11:28

Like an explosion, we saw 17,000 pour out of the stands, nearly crushing us white-faced amigos. Hands went up, waving to the living Jesus, their newfound Friend. Then the Spirit started His healing ministry: eyes opened; ears unstopped; tumors vanished; gums healed; rashes cleared; bones healed. Whoever believed, received! We had taken dominion, and now the Spirit was free to bless.

As we looked up through that hole in the clouds, we easily imagined seeing this same crowd of joyous people seated soon around that great Supper table, praising their newfound Saviour!

Dominion Over Demons

Perhaps there is nothing more terrifying to observe than the torture in a demon-possessed child. Jesus was so upset by the plight of such children, that He declared a terrible judgment against any who caused "one of these little ones to stumble" (*see* Matthew 18:6). Now in the baseball stadium, Satan was prepared to challenge our dominion over his power again.

With screams of anguish, a pretty five-year-old child bolted out of the stands onto the playing field into the group of Americans around the podium. Her arms thrashing aimlessly, legs jerking and jumping, and eyes blazing in hate, she taunted us to do something about it. Four of us grabbed her convulsing body and held her on the ground. As I peered into her brown eyes, they became greenish like a snake's, with a demon looking out at me.

We were to learn later that this was a minister's daughter who for two years had not slept unless drugged. Her constant seizures had started when her father had received the Baptism of the Holy Spirit one night in his study. He was now about ready to crack under the strain of seeing his little girl fail to respond to any medical treatments. The problem was obvious.

If you have never yet felt "righteous indignation," wait till you meet a demon attacking a defenseless child! Your blood will boil. You will roll up your spiritual sleeves and land a haymaker in the name of Jesus!

We did. It took twenty minutes to get that demon's attention. We couldn't get his name, as he kept turning away when he heard "Jesus," "blood," "rebuke," "come out," and "leave her alone."

Suddenly he fled. The child went limp. From her mouth poured a puddle of green foam. The crowd around us handed us tissues and handkerchiefs, as we frantically wiped away the mess, lest she choke. Then her body seemed to come alive, and she looked up with the most beautiful smile, as though returning to friends after a long absence from reality. Her sobbing father folded her in his arms, then led her laughing and skipping to her mother in the stands.

The preacher's work had been done for him. He invited the crowd this night to accept the only Saviour who can make Satan run away. They came forward by the hundreds.

Our "Day Off"

The next day our van took us into the back country. It rolled to a stop under a famous tree, the largest in Guatemala, whose welcome shade covered the open marketplace next to an ancient, earthquake-damaged Catholic cathedral.

It was a beautiful sight, with the native ladies in their colorful flowing garb, preparing their displays of merchandise and produce, homemade and homegrown.

A huge woven display basket full of hundreds of bananas looked enticing. I told the interpreter to have the little old grandma wrap up a dollar's worth for me to take back to the hotel for snacks. Then I moved on to look at the native handcrafts. As I returned, there stood our whole group from the van convulsed with laughter. "You must have gone bananas," one announced. "You bought the whole crop!" Sure enough, one dollar had bought out grandma! Ever after, we have been known as "the Ebys who went bananas in Guatemala."

Dominion Over Gravity

Stopping at the cathedral in Antigua, the ancient capital, we were amazed that it had withstood three major earthquakes over the centuries. One of the sisters proudly pointed to the dozen or so large statues standing in niches hundreds of feet above the courtyard.

"Some people who come here," she said, "do not believe in miracles, so we show them ours. You see those great heavy statues of the saints up there? You see the great cracks in the walls from our earthquakes over more than three hundred years? You see how the whole roof fell in two years ago from that great quake? Well, not one of those statues ever fell. God protects His saints!" Her brown eyes sparkled from under the black hood, and I could read her thoughts: "My Christos will protect me too."

Dominion Over the Airways

Around the corner and up a rutted dirt street, we stopped to see a textile "factory," where children work the looms after they turn five. When they are fifteen, they "graduate" to other work. Outside I saw a group of brown-skinned youngsters whom the interpreter told me were speaking ancient Mayan. The larger boy was explaining about the "Jesus of love" to whom he prayed at the church. The others stood fascinated.

The boy agreed to talk into my recorder which he first handled with amazement, like something from outer space. He said that the villagers had been hearing about Jesus over the few TV sets in town that showed a program in Spanish from America called "Gloria a Dios." He

Dr. Eby records a rare Mayan dialect spoken by these children, who have "heard about Jesus at the cathedral."

said that all the villagers were excited. Many had gone to hear the "Americanos from TV" at the big stadium, but they weren't back yet, since most of them had to walk. Had we heard about those Americans who talk about Jesus? I can still see his smile of joy to learn that we were those people and that he, too, was on our "Jesus team." Jesus had said, "The least of these is the greatest."

Become as Little Children

> ... Verily, I say unto you, Except ye be con-
> verted, and become as little children, ye shall not
> enter into the kingdom of heaven. Whosoever
> therefore shall humble himself as this little child,
> the same is the greatest in the kingdom of
> heaven. And whoso shall receive one such little
> child in my name receiveth me.
>
> Matthew 18:3–5

WHEN DOUBTERS tell me that there are no miracles, I sug-
gest that they look into the eyes of a baby. No great work
of art or literature can equal the eloquence of what we see
there.

I take a look every day: in the nursery, at the supermarket, on the sidewalk, in the playgrounds, at restaurants, in the pews—wherever a little one with thumb in
mouth is searching, searching, searching for someone at
whom he can smile.

And my heart sings at what I see in those eyes of that
little soul, so recently come from Jesus' very presence. No
wonder He told His disciples when they came down from
the mountain: ". . . it is not the will of your Father which
is in heaven, that one of these little ones should perish"
(Matthew 18:14). To prove it, He headed for Jerusalem
and its cross.

I think that Paul must have looked into a child's little face just before he wrote the inspired words: "Who shall separate us from the love of Christ?" I can read that same query in the little eyes of today—no different after twenty centuries:

"Shall tribulation" (tummy aches)?

"Or distress" (runny noses)?

"Or persecution" (impatient parents)?

"Or famine" (bottles too soon empty)?

"Or nakedness" (bare feet on burning sidewalks)?

"Or peril" (sixty miles an hour without seat belts)?

"Or sword" (open pins or nurses' needles)?

Eby's version of Romans 8:35

Then I read further in those beautiful eyes: "No, no, no! Nothing shall separate us from the love of our God— unless it is you out there!"

And I shudder. Can it be true that anyone would want to hurt one of these little messengers of love? Can it be true that grown-up products of our school systems are so depraved that they would beat up kids? Can it be that "adults" are the number-one cause for infant deaths and youthful suicides? Will God stand still for this carnage? Ask Him:

But whoso shall offend one of these little ones which believe in me, it were better for him that a millstone were hanged about his neck, and that he were drowned in the depth of the sea.

Matthew 18:6

I can hear Satan sneer: "Humans are such dupes. God created them to be beautiful, and I talk them into being ugly. He offers them His hand, but they prefer my hate. He gave them His Son, but they prefer my sin. He tells them how to live, but they choose to die. He even gives them love, but they seek lust. I get my kicks out of putting millstones around their necks. I can never figure why they do not object. Aha, aha, what dupes!"

Babes in Harms

Having been a fetus once myself, I must speak out in behalf of that one who this very day is being slaughtered somewhere. I am not alone in abhorring carnage of the innocents. I get sick to my stomach, and so should you, to look into a surgical basin at the pieces of one of God's helpless miracles reduced to a bloody mess. It is like looking in abject horror at the King of Love being nailed again on a cross of dripping gore and torn flesh! A scream sticks in my throat: Why? Why? Why?

Is one of the reasons that causes Jesus the Christ to wretch—vomit unceasingly, spew out of His mouth (*see* Revelation 3:16)—the sight of millions of fetal corpses in *America* annually being mangled in disposals? Is it the knowledge that His very church sits by silently? Is it that the legal tender inscribed "In God We Trust" is being extracted even from home-loving citizens to pay for legalized mayhem? How can God bless America now?

Oh, yes, as an obstetrician, I know the arguments favoring planned parenthood. The original concept was acceptable, that is, to assist _parents_ to have and rear an acceptable number of babies. I fear the concept has been forgotten! Such "planning" is now principally concerned with preliminary prostitution—not in preventing it, but assisting teenagers to find ways "to have sex safely." "Do you need an abortion? Do you need penicillin? We will get it free for you."

You say: "Doc, you're biased." You are so right! I am biased in favor of a society that rejects a return to the morals of Rome, Greece, or Babylon, when Diana's temples of female slavery preceded and produced the collapse of those empires! I am biased in favor of God's way: a body that is a clean temple; a mind that seeks truth not filth; a family who can respect one another; a girl who prefers self-control to syphilis; a boy who wants to be a real man in his future home, not a guilt-ridden escapee from memories he cannot erase.

A Walk With the Doctor

Take a walk with me while I talk to youngsters in our city clinic. (Christians, don't turn off your hearing aids.) First, we go to the parenthood-planning clinic.

"Hey, guy, are you the doc here? Gimmee some more birth pills. I ran out. The Relief won't give me enough dough for me to buy 'em!" The fifteen-year-old ground off the end of her cigarette and stuck the stub behind her ear. "I got to have 'em before I get in bed tonight." She was so casual about it.

"How long have you been on the pill?" I asked.

"Since twelve, I suppose. Y'know, since I was old

enough to get caught. I gotta get some sleep! Can't worry every night, y'know."

I ventured a question: "Did it ever occur to you that you could sleep alone at your age?"

A frown of disbelief at my abysmal ignorance spread across her face. "Hey, guy, I don't know any girl these days who sleeps alone! How can you make out that way? Are you a nut?"

I agreed I was, as the nurse handed the prepackaged pills to her with motherly advice: "Don't run out next time, dearie."

* * *

In the next room a fourteen-year-old sat sobbing—just a slip of a girl, hair obscuring her eyes. "The nurse says my test is positive. I can't believe it! He said he loved me and wouldn't get me pregnant as long as we went steady," she whispered. "He said it was always safe because he had sex three times with other girls on the pill just before he came over for our date. He promised. He promised. I think I'm going to hate him. I'm so scared of an abortion, but my girl friends say it won't hurt. Does it?"

I was about to reply, when the nurse handed her the referral slip to the County Women's Ward.

* * *

"Please hurry, doctor. There are twenty-three girls waiting," the nurse chided me with a shrug.

"Next" turned out to be a twelve-year-old child whose veneer of sophistication was transparent. Her mother, a metabolic disaster of three hundred pounds, dragged her into the examining room. "This is a quickie, Doc," she reassured me. "Her diaphragm's done broke. Just fit her for a new one. She'll probably need two sizes bigger, heh, heh."

I felt nauseated. "Is she your only child, Ma'am?" "Oh, no, Doc. She's my third gal. They all have lots of friends at the house. After school every day, a whole batch of boys come home with them for the parties. You see, they knows I keep my girls protected so they won't get in trouble. I'm a good mother, ain't I, sweetie?" I looked away from the sick grins.

*   *   *

Don't leave yet. You and I have an appointment at the hospital. A skinny, pallid "child," barely seventeen, is lying exhausted from malnutrition and childbirth in the ward next to the nursery. We worry about her newborn.

And we should. Huddled over a listless premature form is the chief of pediatrics who has just left an office-ful of needy children to dash here. He is placing a tiny tubing into the umbilical vessel. Two nurses are adjusting oxygen flow and bassinet heat. The technologist is poised with a lancet to "run blood gases." The X-ray technician is centering the tube over the semi-collapsed chest. A feeble jerking occurs in the little legs. A nurse in the adjoining ward is telling her mother, "Don't worry, the state will pay your bill."

"Another narc baby," explains the discouraged doctor. "Won't high-school kids ever learn? Not a chance: immature, premature, malnourished, drug-saturated—already has withdrawal symptoms. One lung failed to open—acidotic, too. Never had a chance. What a rotten deal for a kid! That angel dust!" I saw him clench a fist.

P.S. An hour later the little soul was welcomed into paradise by a host of real angels who know no dust.

* * *

This is our last case for the day: a prostitute in labor. History: three abortions, syphilis and gonorrhea (treated), now mentally damaged, five years on every available drug by mouth or needle—cocaine, angel dust, speed, weed, alcohol, nicotine. Spent all her money on drugs nine months ago. Missed her pill, then her period. Four months ago she stumbled into a store-front mission near Haight-Ashbury. She heard a new name—*Jesus*. Someone said He loves prostitutes and addicts. She needed that. Someone said: "Believe, He can save you!" She did, and she started laughing for the first time in years. "I suddenly felt free, like I was forgiven," she told me in amazement.

For the past two months at the office, we had prayed together, commanding Satan to take his filthy hands off the baby. We were believing that the Holy Spirit would replace those little damaged organs before birth. "Thank You, Jesus, for that bloody stripe You bore just for this helpless little soul." And now the hour had come.

The labor was relatively short, and the baby greeted us with a cry of joy. Fists clenched; legs kicked; chest heaved with deepening breaths! He was perfect. God had replaced any defects with better-than-good tissues. After all, He has promised to do all things well. Why not believe Him?

We Visit Other Children

"You'll never be the same," they had told us. Our plane was making its descent into Port-au-Prince, Haiti—so beautiful from the air with its crescentic harbor dotted with slumbering ships of commerce.

"Could a loving God really overlook people in such a green oasis in a blue sea?" we asked ourselves. "Of course not," we heard an inner voice reply, "but they could overlook God."

Two hours later we stood with quivering chins in the open-air, fly-filled mess hall at the mission. With skins shining like ebony, and faces lighted with anticipation, three hundred bony but beautiful little street children poured off old buses, down the stairs, onto the benches alongside the wooden tables. "Beggars?" "Urchins?" "Waifs?" Oh, no, Jesus' babies!

We looked into eyes of love which knew love when they saw it—wide eyes, full of wonder. Eyes which had never seen a square meal, and probably wouldn't. Eyes which Jesus had said were of the Kingdom of Heaven. Our own started to tear.

This would be their only meal for four days. Each place setting was the same: a tin cup half-full of reconstituted milk, topped with a layer of flies. A few specks of blackened meat was visible in the small lump of soggy corn-and-wheat mush on each tin plate. With unbelievable self-control they sat, as no one would eat till all were silent. We watched the tiny tots pat their bloated tummies with one hand, while holding a stiff finger to their lips. Then the prayer, in Creole: "We thank You, Jesus, for

"Soulful eyes" in hand-me-down clothes crowd the waiting room, in hopes of being selected for a first-come, first-served milk-and-mush meal.

our daily bread. Amen." The milk disappeared in the first gulps.

The scene was too much. We cried unashamed. Back home in thousands of homes and restaurants, a royal battle was going on over which choice of meats, drinks, and desserts each child would demand, sample, and discard—without even a thought of thanks. Babies would be screaming for grown-up food, and youngsters would be kicking at parents because their favorite soft drink had run out. Bedlam would be the usual dinner-table scene.

We looked down at the seven-year-old beside us. She had carried her three-year-old sister on her back while pulling the four-year-old brother alongside. She ate slowly, watching the other two finish their scoop.

Quietly, she divided her remaining portion in half, and pushed in onto their plates. It was gone in two bites. She would not eat again until next week.

I could see Jesus sitting there with His arms around that bony child: "And again I say, Suffer little children . . . to come unto me. . . (Matthew 19:14). Even a cup of water given in my name will make you rich in heaven (*see* Matthew 10:42).

Satan Is Behind the Whole Mess

It is not a case of "Satan made me do it," but rather a case of "Satan showed me how, and I did it."

Child beating and abuse, famine and desertion, cursing and maligning, cruelty and murder—name any crimes against a fellowman, young or old—all, that's right, all are concocted by Satan.

God's Word has warned us well in advance what to expect of lukewarm men today: "Now the Spirit speaketh expressly, that in the lattertimes some [humans] shall depart from the faith, giving heed to seducing spirits, and doctrines of devils; Speaking lies in hypocrisy; having their conscience seared with a hot iron" (1 Timothy 4:1, 2). Then Satan begins roaming the earth seeking whom he can find to devour like a roaring lion.

You still doubt that mankind is carrying out Satan's offstage directives? Read some of God's Word about our perilous times in these last days. This reads like your morning *Times:*

> For men shall be lovers of their own selves, covetous, boasters, proud, blasphemers, disobedient to parents,

unthankful, unholy, Without natural affection, truce-breakers, false accusers, incontinent, fierce, despisers of those that are good, Traitors, heady, highminded, lovers of pleasures more than lovers of God; Having a form of godliness, but denying the power thereof: *from such turn away.* For of this sort are they which creep into houses, and lead captive silly women laden with sins, led away with divers lusts, Ever learning, and never able to come to the knowledge of the truth!

2 Timothy 3:2–7, *italics added*

It is really no different in Haiti than here at home. Satan is the prince of the powers of the air (temporarily), and both nations have air! Here at home, we are simply more cleverly disguising sins which God predicted for these days. There we can hear the voodoo drums, beating a dirgelike chant to Satan. We can view the elaborately painted shrines to Satan and his supposed-holy mother. We can scarcely press through the crowds of aimless street people from whom Satan has stolen all hope of future, food, or fair play.

There we can see bloated, starved street babies sucking on garbage from the gutters. Here, where Satan is more often disguised as an angel of light, we feed our street babies X-rated garbage. We let our aimless street masses wander without knowing there *is* hope of a future, food, and fair play if they accept Jesus. There the results of man's abuse of man are a way of life. Here it is taught on TV in case any of our "innocents" have failed to discover where the life-style is really at! We're *so* clever.

Satan + Helpers = The Mess We're In

Why are millions of children starving across God's favored earth? Did the Creator create too little tillable soil? Did He limit the ability of His vegetation to bring forth seed? Did He create Man to be a dumb animal, blind to his own family's needs? Did He create the wombs merely to fill tombs? God forbid!

What God did create was a fabulously complex triune man, *with a will to choose!* What He also created was a Lucifer with a will which rebelled. When the two creations got together, they decided to do things their way. The results? Chaos.

You doubt me? What about God's record? It says:

Genesis 3:	Adam and Eve + Satan = death for man
1 Kings 12:	Jeroboam + Satan = golden calves
John 13:27:	Judas + Satan = betrayal of Christ
Job 2:5:	man + Satan = cursing God
Luke 4:7:	power + Satan = deceit
John 8:44:	man + Satan = lusts and lies
1 Peter 5:8:	man + Satan = devouring lion
Luke 13:16:	woman + Satan = eighteen–year infirmity
Luke 4:35:	man + devil = seizures and blasphemy

Luke 22:31:   Peter + Satan = denial of
                      Jesus

Revelation 12:7–9:   Michael + Satan = war in
                      heaven (defeat for Satan)

Revelation 13:2, 7:   Beast + Satan = blasphemy,
                      war on saints

Then: Revelation 20:10: God vs. Satan = casting into
                         the lake of fire

Joy Cometh in the Morning

We have read the end of the Book. There *is* a final victory. It is in Jesus, the King of Kings, the Conqueror!

He has set the stage. He has chosen the players. He has directed the plot. He has never forgotten, much less forsaken, His children—no matter what age. Each is precious. For them He is busy preparing the Supper.

In the meantime, what? We pray and aid all children—little, fat or hungry, found or lost. We go into all the world, either in person or through our support of those who can serve the needy. We put all our talents to work where the Holy Spirit leads us. We share till it hurts God's measureless blessings of time, energy, and brains which He has showered among His children here! Then we resist the devil and anything he sponsors. We come against that tricky tyrant with our two-edged sword of the Spirit. God says this is part of our commission in being His ambassadors in these last days. He makes it so simple. He says, "Follow Me. Become My child. You will soon be home for Supper."

It is exciting when we know we win.

He Will Abundantly Pardon

> Seek ye the Lord while he may be found, call ye
> upon him while he is near: Let the wicked forsake
> his way, and the unrighteous man his thoughts:
> and let him return unto the Lord, and he will
> have mercy upon him; and to our God, for he will
> abundantly pardon. For my thoughts are not your
> thoughts, neither are your ways my ways, saith
> the Lord.
>
> Isaiah 55:6–8

WE COULD SCARCELY believe that our bags were being checked for Korea. Another wonder! We would see what God hath wrought in the few years since Seoul had been 93 percent leveled by war. We would find the answer to its sudden emergence as the world's finest community of Christians.

We could not have been more surprised. In a city of many millions, none were unemployed. People scurried along the streets, ever bowing to each other, in a spirit of civic pride and personal respect. Skyscrapers were ultramodern. An underground "city" of stores offered merchandise from around the world. Colorful clothing merged with the artistry of buildings and courtyards as we bused through city and countryside. These people truly had spirit! We had come from great big America to share with these people, and now it was obvious they would bless us!

We soon learned that Jesus had preceded us to this "uttermost part of the earth," far from Jerusalem. That was the answer to Seoul's remarkable rebirth. Out of the disaster and despair of war, He had raised up human hands and hearts in praise to Him. They had read 2 Chronicles 7:14 and had believed what it said: ". . . I will hear from heaven . . . and will heal their land." In fact, they were believing *everything* that God said!

On a man-made island stands a cluster of large and tall buildings, housing the world's largest assemblage of Christians—nearly one hundred thousand strong. Like the others, we arrived by bus, one of hundreds chartered every Sunday by the neighborhood prayer groups to get them to church, in hopes of finding a seat at one of the four morning services. The pastor relies upon the fifty-seven hundred group leaders to get each "block flock" to and from church, since very few Koreans can afford a car.

Visitors from America, where smaller churches are scarcely peopled on Sundays, stand in awe as they watch the overflow crowds turned into adjoining buildings, after the first twelve thousand are seated, or squeezed, into the main sanctuary, service after service. Then in the evening, each member is expected to bring an unsaved newcomer. For non-Koreans the balcony seats are equipped with headphones tuned to skilled interpreters, speaking in four languages.

From the balcony we noted that each Korean had come

Christians in Seoul crowd Dr. Cho's 10,000-seat church building for one of the four Sunday services.

equipped with Bible and pencil which was placed on a
ledge for easy writing. Ten thousand pencils circled
verses, as Dr. Cho quoted from God's promises. When he
prayed, twenty thousand hands reached skyward to
touch the Jesus of life and miracles. The arched dome
echoed the choir's praises like a reply from angels. The
collection plates overflowed with "widow's mites" given
from hearts thankful for answered prayers. The hovering,
covering Spirit of God lay like thick incense over those
humble heads.

As Americans, we were learning a needed lesson.

Prayer Mountain

"How do you explain this phenomenal church?" we
asked an assistant pastor. "We'll show you tomorrow,"

he said. "It is no secret now, because Jesus told His children how to prosper: 'pray without ceasing' and 'believe that you have what you asked.' It does require humility, but we have plenty after our war."

There is nothing like it in America. Prayer Mountain lies several miles north of Seoul's outskirts and represents the "front line" for Dr. Cho's worshiping warriors. Besides a large one-story building, where a thousand fasting, praying worshipers lie on mats for days at a time communing with God on behalf of lost souls, the mountainside is pockmarked with scores of cryptlike prayer rooms dug into the slanting hill. Each is cemented, with a door and outside ledge for one's doffed shoes or sandals. One, at most two, church members can remain here closeted for prayer and fasting in the quietness of solitary

A Prayer Mountain "cell" north of Seoul. Sandals on the door ledge indicate an intercessor at prayer inside. More than 1,200 a day walk to the mountain to talk to God.

meditation on God's Word. The sounds of nearby construction of additional worship centers do not reach their ears. They are there to hear Jesus.

In this peaceful place, we all but forget that back in the city the ten-story Missions Center at the church is providing the crowds of local and visiting workers with advanced studies in all phases of preaching and teaching the Word, in various languages. They are training missionaries to carry the Good News about Jesus' love—even to America, since it seems not to have heard it lately.

We had seen prayer at work. We had seen humble, poor people, by our standards, believing exactly whatever God said in His Book. We could see the results. From a group of a few families huddled under a tent fif-

"Of such is the kingdom of heaven." Little hearts and hands praise the tender Jesus during the sidewalk Sunday-school lesson.

teen years ago has grown a born-again body of Christians, one hundred thousand strong, sending missionaries abroad to share the Word that it is simply wonderful to call upon the Lord while He is near and may yet be found.

They have found Him as the Source of their daily bread. Whether in huts, hovels, or houses, He is all they need. They know war; they know human politics. And they know the difference that Jesus has made whenever they have gotten on their knees and have had a conversation with Him. We had seen His wisdom at work in Korea.

Next Stop—Hong Kong

Busy, busy, busy. Cars, trucks, buses, and pushcarts. Hillside apartments reaching to the sky. Tightly compressed shops, factories, tenements. Rusty shipyards. Acres of undulating boat people. Thousands of refugees in packing-box camps. Eight million stomachs seeking nourishment, and sixteen million feet on the move. Very few have found their answers. Who is to tell them?

In three days, what can be seen and said about Hong Kong? Just as people everywhere, they are searching for the solution to survival, and therefore, they belong in either of two camps—those who have found, or those who still need, Jesus!

We took a bus ride to the border of Red China where signs warn against trespassing beyond that point. We detained our bodies there but sent the Spirit across the rice

We find China's frontier closed, but not to the power of prayer. Red China produced a spiritual vacuum that our God is filling with hope, comfort, and love.

fields with the fervent prayer that He would soften Red hearts with His limitless mercy and would create in them a new spirit of love for their Redeemer. The prayers are working. China is being opened to new ideas, and one of them will be a God, not of ivory, but of flesh, who has borne their cares, has bled in their place.

A highlight for anyone is a nighttime cruise on the *Glory Boat* as it slips quietly through the harbor between the shores lined with compacted vertical "cities of lighted windows." Then it moves back and forth through the city of rocking boat people on their lifelong waterbed. A few shout greetings, others just warnings. We are told why.

It seems that God made this old boat available to the American missionary two or three years ago for carrying the Good News among the myriad junks and sampans in the harbor. Young people came aboard out of curiosity and joy over the novel music they heard. Chinese boys and girls were singing and playing into microphones, telling of a new God—one who is alive and well, without dragon teeth, but with a heart of love. For some, it was the greatest story they'd ever heard; for others, it sounded like a lie.

Then in 1979 God decided to open Red China for some reason—for a good reason. He had prepared an advance guard of Hong Kong Chinese youths to carry His Good News across the border. With them went His Word in tracts, cassettes, and parts of Bibles. When they left, the

God had made the Glory Boat available to carry the Good News among the junks and sampans in the harbor. In the darkness, this old boat has already brought a shaft of light to discouraged hearts in the harbor.

word about Jesus was to be filtered from house to house
and paddy to paddy. Little hand-cranked generators
would grind through the nighttime as cassette players
told of a coming day when Jesus would rule in their
hearts.

The *Glory Boat* may have seen its day, but it has
pointed many souls toward the day of glory!

Indonesia and Mel Tari

Our TBN Crusaders' prayers had been centered upon
Jakarta during this '79 tour. Our Indonesian evangelist
had already introduced thousands of TV watchers on that
huge island to the faces of Paul and Jan Crouch, and
others of us. Mel Tari had readied the huge stadium and
hungry hearts for our message about a loving God.

We will seldom again meet more gracious people.
Though their stature was small, their smiles were mighty.
Only a few spoke English, but it didn't seem to matter.
Whether from the slums or the slate-roofed suburbs, we
all seemed as one. Life seemed to mingle everywhere,
even on the streets where bicycles, pushcarts, souped-up
golf carts, and metro buses all used the same lanes and
barely missed one another. Behind our swank hotel, we
watched a refugee, fishing in a garbage-laden creek while
he sat on the riverbank of the tiled-roof hacienda next
door.

Upstairs in the hotel, we were having a problem. The
new sixty-five-hundred-dollar TV camera refused to
work. Our TV tech had tried every suggestion in the

A new TV camera + Satan = no picture. A new TV camera + prayer = no Satan.

manual since leaving Los Angeles. Nothing was wrong with the circuits. It just wouldn't work!

That was reason enough for Paul and Jan to go to work. They phoned four of us to converge on that room, where we found the floor, the bed, table and chairs covered with TV parts, tools, and assorted spares. The cameraman was sweating, from heat and exhaustion. We laid hands on various parts.

"All right, Satan," Paul announced. "We've had enough of you! We came to proclaim Jesus' power and to show the world the miracles He is going to perform. In the name of Jesus, I take authority over you, and so do all of these children of God! You are to take your hands off this equipment this minute. It is God's property, not yours. I rebuke you in Jesus' name. Now go! Amen and praise the Lord!"

We looked at each other. We felt at peace about this problem. The technician started reassembling the shiny components, and we left.

Ten minutes later, the phone rang again: "Believe it or not, I just plugged it in, and the camera works perfectly. Praise the Lord!" Incidentally, it is still working perfectly months later. And the TV footage has been seen around the globe, blessing those who shared the recorded miracles.

Jesus Is Lord

The Saturday-night crowd filled the stadium as twenty-five thousand sang, clapped, or raised their hands in joy as our TV ministers shared God's News in song and word. It made little difference that we spoke no Indonesian. When necessary, Mel Tari interpreted, but they knew what we meant, somehow. They didn't want us to stop. They were hearing about a Jesus who once died for them and was returning soon to meet them in person. More. More.

Then Mel invited them to accept Jesus' offer of salvation: "Come down to the podium, and I will lead you in a little prayer of repentance, and He will save you!"

Have you ever seen famished people when bread arrives? As if time were running out, we watched fifteen thousand Indonesians race down the aisles, out of the stands, running to be first to pray! They sought out our

Doc and Mel Tari: "You, too, can have this Jesus in your heart. He is Lord! Glor-r-ry!"

Paul and Jan: "We bring greetings from the Christians in America. We are all *one* in the Spirit."

twenty-five American visitors and practically crushed us as they prayed to be touched, healed, and saved. A dozen hands at once pulled at my sweat-soaked shirt, as their eyes begged: "We want your Jesus—now!"

For all of us Americans, this was a new experience. We had not before now seen the total excitement which results when childlike faith first learns that a mighty God's love is available to save and to heal. In America we were used to people who must be begged over and over to discard prejudices and pride long enough to find a personal Saviour.

These Indonesians had not before known that the Great Father of the universe saves and heals just by trusting and loving Him. It was so simple that they couldn't wait to get to the platform. Their only concern seemed to be that Jesus might withdraw His offer before they could pray with us: "Yes, I want You as Saviour and Lord—right now!"

And Jesus Said, "Be Healed"

Have you ever felt the Spirit of God at work when hearts are open to His power? We did that night! Those who have seen the TV footage from Jakarta can now imagine what we sensed.

Suddenly shouts of amazed delight began ringing out across the crowd, as the Holy Spirit searched and found receptive hearts and needy bodies. Our partners were laying on hands as fast as they could anoint a brow: "In the name of Jesus, be healed." The Spirit was touching

"Be healed, in Jesus' name!" The amazed husband gazes at his recovered wife.

humble souls, right and left. I saw Maybelle touch a blind girl, and heard the girl's squeal of amazed delight as she saw light, then faces and people. At the same time, another's ears were opened.

Mel was touching a depressed soul and ordering her spirit of sorrow to go. It did. She jumped with sudden joy. Paul was praying for a stroke victim with a useless arm when it suddenly received new life and shot upward in obedient praise to God. He and Jan centered prayers on a blind and deaf man, only to discover he was demon possessed. "In the name of Jesus come out of him," I heard them say. The camera recorded the miracle, as the demon fled, and the wild blinded eyes received their sight, and ears opened. Everywhere people were receiving the fulfillment of Jesus' promise: "Lay on hands, in My name, and they will recover."

Of the dozens of healings in which I was sharing in my corner of the crowd, I shall not forget the sallow young man being brought by two counselors who had spotted him on a bench. To me, a physician, he appeared to be dying right there. I checked his pulse—irregular at 180 beats, barely palpable, fibrillating. His face was ashen; his pupils dilated; his breath gasping. "He's supposed to be in the hospital tonight for emergency heart surgery," the interpreter informed me. "He trusts God to heal him tonight."

Quickly, I cupped his clammy head in my hands and prayed, "Jesus, please take over before it is too late. Heart, be healed."

I opened my eyes to see him suddenly stiffen as his limp arms lifted themselves toward heaven. His eyes were set. He was unconscious—"slain" in the Spirit, as we say—but standing up! The crowd drew away in hushed surprise. For several minutes, as I ministered to a dozen others, he stood motionless, scarcely breathing.

Then he "melted." His color turned pink, his eyes opened, and the pupils contracted. A smile of wonderment formed, as tears flowed. I caught his wrists to check the pulse. It was seventy-two, regular. His carotid was now strong. He had a new heart. Jesus had operated while he stood! I could hear him shouting to his friends in Indonesian as he pushed through the tightening crowd, "Isn't God good?"

Come Out of Him

> And in the synagogue there was a man, which
> had a spirit of an unclean devil, and cried out
> with a loud voice, Saying, Let us alone; what have
> we to do with thee, thou Jesus of Nazareth? art
> thou come to destroy us? I know thee who thou
> art; the Holy One of God. And Jesus rebuked
> him, saying, Hold thy peace, and come out of
> him. And when the devil had thrown him in the
> midst, he came out of him, and hurt him not.
>
> Luke 4:33–35

FEW PEOPLE TALK about devils these days, except in their
jokes. Satan likes it that way. He wants his demons left
alone to function undisturbed. After all, Satan does not
want his employees destroyed—only the people they de-
ceive! Satan has memorized God's Book and knows that
he and his hordes will end up in chains and pits and a
lake of fire; so why not take every person he can with him
to hell? People don't seem to mind where they go anyway. Besides, he argues, his demons need places to live
where it is warm and protected. Why not *in* people? They
make such good puppets for clever imps. The takeover
is so easy!

Those "Stinking" Spirits

The Bible calls them *unclean* for a good reason: they are. Everything about them is rotten: their smell, their lifestyle, their morals, their language, their techniques, and even their results. They even look hideous to the thousands of liberated souls who have seen them leave in fright when they hear the name they fear above all names. That is the one name under heaven given among men whereby we must be saved. (The demons looked it up in Acts 4:12.)

Satan and his demons also know why Jesus of Nazareth came down to earth where man has put them in charge of world affairs. They try to keep people from finding out, although it is quite easy. Just don't let them read 1 John 3:8. Have you? They do not want their puppets to learn that Jesus came to destroy the works of the devil. Oh, no!

They especially object to anyone's becoming a feared child of God. The idea totally infuriates demons—and for a good reason. A child of God is apt to accept one of God's promises. The demons have read this already in 1 John 4:4, and it even frightens the devil. The promise says: "Ye are of God, little children, and have overcome them [demons]: because greater is he [God] that is in you, than he [Satan] that is in the world."

Then, to make it worse for these frightened demons, God's Word goes on to make unacceptable threats to all demons' security. They have read about these children of God in 1 John 3 and 4 where the Word promises them that "God heareth us" and "whatsoever we ask, we receive of Him," and we "do those things that are pleasing in his sight" (*see* 1 John 4:6; 3:22). Horrors!

The Word even says, "Perfect love casteth out fear that hath torments" (*see* 1 John 4:18). That eliminates the demons' best weapon. Worse yet, the Word goes on to say about these children that ". . . God dwelleth in us, and his love is perfected in us. Hereby, know we that we dwell in him, and he in us, because he hath given us of his Spirit" (1 John 4:12, 13).

That does it for a demon! He is being evicted from his possessed body where he had been the "in" thing. He screams in terror whenever a child of God has boldly declared that his body is now the temple of the Living God, not of an unclean spirit! What will sneaky Satan say about this turn of events?

For such a demon, the war is going badly. But he won't give up. He'll sneak back later with seven other dirtier demons and try to move in again. After all, Jesus had said it could happen in a wicked generation (*see* Matthew 12:45), and Jesus should know. Even demons know He is the Son of God (*see* Matthew 8:29).

Victory Over Unclean Spirits

And when he had called unto him his twelve disciples, he gave them power against unclean spirits, to cast them out, and to heal all manner of sickness and all manner of disease.

Matthew 10:1

Hallelujah! The war is won. Only the mop-up operation remains for God's children to enjoy. Jesus has even given His children the advance report that they are more than conquerors through Him! Who would swap ranks for that born loser Satan after hearing Jesus say, "Well done, thou good and faithful servant?"

Job Description for Believers

Jesus' manual of procedure
for eternal success:

1. And as ye go, preach, saying, The kingdom of heaven is at hand.

    Matthew 10:7

2. Heal the sick, cleanse the lepers, raise the dead. . . .

    Matthew 10:8

3. . . . cast out devils. . . .

    Matthew 10:8

4. . . . freely ye have received, freely give.

    Matthew 10:8

5. . . . take no thought how or what ye shall speak: for it shall be given you in that same hour what ye shall speak.

    Matthew 10:19

Jesus did not say: "Go if you want to"; "Heal if you want to"; "Cast out devils if you want to"; "Preach and teach if you want to." Jesus did not give His followers ". . . over all the power of the enemy . . ." (Luke 10:19) for it to be ignored, discarded, or worse yet, scorned!

Jesus gave to us who bear His name all this power to be used as His ambassador-servants while we are awaiting His return. We have His power of attorney. We have His protection: "... nothing shall by any means hurt you" (Luke 10:19). We have His Spirit, as Comforter and Instructor! We have His armor, and His sword! With all this, we have victory in Christ Jesus, assured in advance. And to show how totally He loves us, He then surrounds us with His guardian angels when we get off our knees and stride into battle!

Two Illustrations of Our Battles

Some time back, my wife and I decided to follow Jesus' *Manual of Procedure*, and to act like King's kids. We were excited about the Good News of Jesus' invitation to "come" then "go," to "believe" then "receive," to "lift up hands" then "lay on hands," to "die to self" then "live for God." When Jesus had us ready, He opened the door, and we were off and running—right into Satan!

What a collision! That dirty turkey was out to destroy our testimony, our enthusiasm, our security, and even our health. But we won! Jesus bound up our wounds and gave us His joy. We were given new friends from God's family. We have received new strength, new boldness, new peace, and we have just gotten started. Read on for highlights of our battles.

Case One: Sirens

We will not forget the day which Satan had picked for Maybelle's death! He did not like what she had been telling audiences of mothers and children about a loving Lord Jesus. He struck unexpectedly as she sat under a hair dryer, sharing about Jesus with another lady waiting to become beautiful.

I was at home typing when the phone rang: "We've called the ambulance. Your wife has had a heart attack. They'll have her at the hospital in a few minutes." The phone went dead, and I grabbed my car keys.

In moments, at my hospital, I had the ICU team readied for Maybelle's arrival. Then we waited, and waited. Frantically, I phoned the beauty shop and was told that she should have arrived. Little did I suspect that an out-of-town ambulance had been called, because all local units were tied up. Nor could I yet know that the crew had refused to take my wife to my hospital because they had a contract to take all patients to another hospital. With her semiconscious gasps and Swedish stubbornness, she had finally forced them to turn around and take their helpless victim to me and her waiting cardiologist.

When she finally arrived, she looked like a goner. Gasping, gray blue, and gurgling on the stretcher, she tried to speak to me: "Daddy—I—love—you! Don't let—me—die. Pray—" And she was unconscious.

I clenched my fists and silently screamed: "You dirty devil, you! Take your stinkin' hands off my wife! You can't have her! She is God's property! In the name of Jesus, I take authority over you and all your demons. I bind you. Jesus binds you! Let her go right now. Jesus' blood has already healed her. I will come against you all my life for what you are doing to her today. Now get lost!

You're defeated in Jesus' name! Thank You, Jesus," I added, "for giving her back to me. We love You."

The ICU team was working frantically. It still looked like the devil would win. I knew that she had never had any heart trouble, and that this must be one of Satan's tantrums made to look like congestive failure. I kept praying.

Later, I was to learn that Maybelle was, at that moment, seeing a vision. As she had slipped into the unconscious stupor of hypoxia, she describes seeing the form of an angel descending to her bed. He cupped his beautiful wings, tip to tip, and cradled her body ever so tenderly. She saw him smile as he whispered: "I'm here to take care of you, Maybelle. Now sleep." Her miracle had happened!

After the attack, her EKG shows a normal, healthy heart. Her cardiologist simply says, "I can't explain it." Satan had lost again!

Case Two: Blasphemy

Geraldine was writhing in pain on a neighbor's sofa when my pastor and I arrived. The long-haired attractive teenager appeared to me, as a physician, to have a ruptured abdominal organ. She was clutching her abdomen, which seemed to be hard and swollen. Her face was distorted, and her teeth clenched. As we approached her, she screamed at us, "They're going to kill me; they are killing me!"

I looked at her eyes staring, wild and threatening. I

knew a demon was looking back at me. "You have a demon?" we asked.

"No, not one, three," she hissed back. "Don't talk to us about that Jesus. He's a fake and a liar. Besides, He's dead, dead, dead. He's bad, bad, bad. He can't help me either." She screamed again in pain. We were listening to her demons speaking through her mouth. It was not her voice!

We did what Jesus had commanded of His followers. We cast those dirty demons out. How? We pleaded the blood of Jesus, and in His name ordered them to leave the girl's body. After about twenty minutes of listening to the name of Jesus being repeated, while they hissed every blasphemy against God that they could conceive, they fled, leaving the girl collapsed on the sofa. Slowly, her color and strength returned. Smiles and tears of relief and joy covered her face. Then she told her awful story.

For only one reason do I repeat her story: I pray that some other gullible teenager may read and avoid a similar pitfall.

At thirteen she was restless, searching for thrills and power. A "friend" suggested she investigate séances at a local "metaphysics church." She felt important when they offered her a spirit all her own to be her companion and instructor. Then, she was given two more. She talked with them by name, and they took over. By fifteen they had convinced her that real dedication and satisfaction in her "church" would require sex on the altar. It sounded exciting at first, but now at seventeen four years of sin had left her hollow and disgusted.

A friend had been praying for her release when six weeks ago she had found Jesus as her Saviour. Then the trouble started. Hideous voices taunted her. She heard her Jesus blasphemed, even in her sleep. She was told that her demon "friends" would kill her unless she renounced God. And tonight they were trying. But prayer and Jesus' name won out—as they always will! Jesus had rescued a lost sheep. What a Friend we have in Jesus.

P.S. We see her often at churches and rallies. She is radiant, joy filled, victorious, and truly liberated as only Jesus can set a prisoner free.

Case Three: Spirit of Defeat

As the healing line formed at the front of a crowded auditorium, we recognized the shaggy-haired bedraggled youth who had sobbed with joy in the morning service when he had found Jesus as his (only?) Friend. He was leading, half-pulling a sad-looking, hollow-eyed woman down the aisle.

"My mother, she needs my Jesus," he explained as he hugged her. "Don't you, mom?" Her haunted eyes searched my face. I smiled, "Tonight Jesus is asking you to let Him be your Friend. Will you?"

"I want to, but my inside voice won't let me. It has been with me for twenty-eight years and keeps telling me never to listen to anything about God. It runs my life." By now she was sobbing in abject defeat—a pitiful sight.

I was getting angry again. I hate demons who destroy people. I pointed my finger, ordered the demon to leave, and saw her thrown violently to the cement floor. This demon meant business. If he should lose this battle, it would be over her dead body. Her body convulsed like a grand-mal seizure. Her eyes were set, pupils dilated. Then came the screaming and cursing. Frightened worshipers retreated up the aisles while four of us fell across her body to protect her from harm.

"Name yourself," I demanded, "and come out of her!" "I am Ee-Oh, Ee-Oh, Ee-Oh," the inside voice screamed back at me and my wife as we tried to hold her thrashing body still.

"All right, Ee-Oh, in the name of Jesus, get out and go to the pit! The blood of Jesus has defeated you. You can't have this child. She belongs to God. Out!"

Suddenly, as though injected with a sedative, the body went limp. Ee-Oh had fled.

We stood up and watched her come back to life, her new life. Color filled her face, tears of release flowed over her cheeks, and a joyous smile spread over her eyes as they saw her son stoop to hug her quieted frame.

Quietly, we all said the sinner's prayer together. We could feel Jesus standing there, with His hand on their heads, just loving her and her reborn son whose newfound faith that day had led his mom to his wonderful Friend. We could all but hear the angels clapping!

The Bottom Line

Jesus ordered every disciple to cast out devils as part of His commission to spread the Good News. We learned that in Matthew 10:8. It is exciting and rewarding work to see the Spirit liberate prisoners from satanic bondage. Yet, Jesus issued a stern warning to you and me when He cautioned His first disciples: ". . . rejoice not, that the spirits are subject unto you; but rather rejoice, because your names are written in heaven," because Jesus explained, ". . . no man knoweth . . . who the Father is, but the Son, and he to whom the Son will reveal him . . . . Blessed are the eyes which see the things that ye see" (Luke 10:20, 22, 23). Then Jesus reminded them that their power over demons originally had been made possible by His casting Satan out of heaven.

Truly our joy is in the Lord as we watch Him at work. In Him do we meditate day and night. To Him belongs all the glory, and power, and honor, now and forevermore. Hallelujah!

I Have Put My Words in Thy Mouth

> But the Lord said unto me, Say not, I am a child:
> for thou shalt go to all that I shall send thee, and
> whatsoever I command thee thou shalt speak. Be
> not afraid of their faces: for I am with thee to de-
> liver thee, saith the Lord. Then the Lord put forth
> his hand, and touched my mouth. And the Lord
> said, Behold, I have put my words in thy mouth.
>
> Jeremiah 1: 7–9

I MUST SHARE WITH you one of the most amazing and blessed events of my life. Its impact upon your life, I pray, will be as excitingly important as God meant it for me. To tell this story properly, I must set the scene which was conceived by a loving Jehovah a long time ago.

Setting the Plan

For *me* to become involved, God had to wait until July of 1979 when certain persons' paths would cross. For *God* to become involved, He had to be attacked by Lucifer early in eternity, change his adversary's name to Satan, and cast that liar to earth. At the same time, God made plans to send part of Himself to earth someday to resume a holy reign there and to restore His children to their birthright in His family. The complete story is told in His Bible.

God's part of the plan was beautiful. He so loved the world that He would send His very Son in the form of man to pay the ransom, which Satan demanded after kidnapping the race, and to establish a kingdom of righteousness to bless all men with eternal love, liberty, and life.

Man's reaction was to destroy the plan. He wanted no part of righteousness. It might spoil his fun of being his own boss so he could continuously have thoughts of evil. Consequently, he spat on the Man, the King of the Jews, beat His flesh from His bones, hanged Him on a cross, and defiantly sealed His tomb. In his fury, however, little man overlooked a big detail: *the plan was eternal.* Jesus had said, ". . . I will come again, and receive you unto myself; that where I am, there ye may be also" (John 14:3).

Today Jesus is ready! He has seen the unwitting nations fulfill every one of His Father's prophecies relative to the plan, most of them in the last three decades. Jesus can now see His chosen (to be witnesses) people collecting in their own (twice) Promised Land. He sees ten European nations ready to assume world government. He sees wars and human hate ready to explode into *the war.* He sees human hearts failing for fear. He sees demon worship becoming fashionable. He sees finances, food, and families failing worldwide. He sees world suicide on the horizon. And above all, He sees the answer: Himself, the worthy Lamb!

His Announcement

"Surely, I come quickly . . ." (Revelation 22:20). Jesus said this to His disciples many times in many ways, and they reported His promise as a major part of His will that He made out for His joint heirs. He has said: "Listen, watch, wait." He is about to say to His angel Gabriel: "Blow the trumpet!" He merely is awaiting His Father's uplifted hand to give the signal for Him to descend in clouds to receive His born-again body of believers both out of paradise and from the earth. Then He will train them as His "kings and priests," administrators and ministers, to rule with Him after He sets foot on the Mount of Olives. What an announcement! But there's more.

A favorite expression used by one of my evangelist friends when he reports a new miracle is "Hang onto your seat belts." Well, grab hold! Here comes the story of how Jesus involved me once again in His plan.

My Encounter

In mid-July of 1979 I had found it impossible to get a return airplane ticket to California from Norfolk, Virginia, where I was scheduled for a "700 Club" TV appearance. Excuses were plentiful: downed DC-10s, inadequate substitute seats, changed air schedules between coasts, and so on. I would simply have to lay over a day, they said. It became clear that the Lord wanted me there an extra day. But why? I would soon know.

That morning the TV program was Spirit *saturated!* Praises flowed, phones replied, spectators were "slain" and healed. The studio felt drenched in God's power, as He ministered to millions of unseen viewers. I felt that something new was happening. Then we moved into a meeting room jam packed with hundreds of the station's administrators and employees, singing and praising just for joy! The Spirit seemed to fall in waves for the next two hours as prayers poured heavenward, binding Satan and freeing the airways for a renewed revival around the world! I knew that something *big* was about to happen.

About then I heard the young studio chauffeur whisper, "It's time to return you to the hotel for lunch." En route I asked him if he would get any sleep that night. "No, I must pick up someone at the private airstrip between one and two in the morning—someone called 'Arthur.' " Instantly, I heard that still small voice within me say: "Now you know. You're here to meet Arthur Blessitt. Be there!"

Reflexly, I blurted out: "I'll go with you. Do you know Arthur's last name?"

"I think they said 'Blessed' or 'Blessit,' something like that. Do you know him?" he replied.

"I should say so; he's one of my dearest friends! I had no idea he was not in California today! What a surprise to run into him here."

"I'll bet he'll be surprised, too," replied the chauffeur, "especially, in the middle of the night!"

About 1:15 A.M. the little Piper touched down and taxied toward our van. When Arthur was a yard from me, I yelled our favorite greeting: "Praise the Lord, Arthur!" He froze in amazed disbelief and blurted, "Not *you*, Doc!

Not four thousand miles from California! Not in the middle of the night! It's a miracle!" In the darkness, with tears of joy, we hugged each other, realizing that this was no chance encounter.

As the van headed for the hotel, Arthur fell to his knees and grabbed mine. Sobs of holy joy and humility shook his frame. His voice rose in praise to his Father.

The van became filled with the heavy presence of the Holy Spirit as we both communed with God. Then he abruptly looked into my bowed face: "Doc," he sobbed in joy, "the Spirit says that you are to anoint me right now for the purpose for which Jesus has called me. You know, He is calling me to announce that the glory of the coming of the Lord is *at hand!*"

In shocked surprise I spoke to the Lord: "Why me? I have no oil. I don't know the words that would please You!"

I found my hand on Arthur's brow, and I heard myself say, "In the name of Jesus, our Almighty God and Saviour, I hereby anoint you, Arthur, for the task and purpose for which He has called you this night. May His wisdom, love, and power overflow you constantly as you carry out your commission and calling in His name! Amen and hallelujah!"

As my tongue went silent, the van slowed to a stop at the side of the highway. I looked up to see why. The chauffeur who told me earlier in the day that he was only recently born again, was slumped over the arm of his seat, "slain" in the Spirit, sobbing in prayer, with hands uplifted. To me it felt like waves of heat as the Spirit filled that vehicle with His Presence for the next several moments. Heaven was near. Then the Spirit seemed to lift, the driver turned the key, and we found ourselves at the hotel, still overawed and even physically shaken by the power which had overshadowed us.

"Arthur," I said as we stepped from the van, "do you realize that this is already July nineteenth, and that you are to be the first guest on today's program? Do you realize that you will be heard around the world? Do you realize that only yesterday at the studio the Spirit witnessed to hundreds of us that Jesus is accelerating every ministry that carries His Good News of salvation to the uttermost parts of His earth? And He is returning so soon now that He is pouring out His Spirit as never before? And this month initiates a stage in His plan to "do a new thing" suddenly, because He is on His way?

I saw a look of surprised realization spread over his face. His penetrating eyes fixed on mine as a smile of sudden joy accented his words: "Doc, that's right! I will be able to tell about His love as never before! Isn't God good! O Jesus, make me worthy; use me!"

Sequel

It is happening. Every man of God whom I have lately contacted reports the same thing—a sudden hunger has gripped the hearts of people around the world. We all can report a sudden increase in the size of standing-room-only crowds wherever the fullness of the beautiful Good News of Jesus' love is being proclaimed. People are suddenly finding in Jesus the answers to lifelong needs. Invitations to receive Him as their personal Saviour are suddenly being eagerly accepted. Souls and bodies are being healed as signs of His faithful promises. Families are being reunited, addicts are being freed, as sins are forgiven, and sorrows turned to joy.

Suddenly, millions of sin-scarred souls are turning their eyes upon Jesus and looking full in His wonderful face, as the things of earth grow strangely dim in the light of His glory and grace. Hallelujah!

Jesus Challenges You

The only God who lives and loves is urging you, "Come up hither." He is saying to you, "Simply take a good look at heaven's advantages, at eternal life with the only Almighty Father, at the benefits of having a constant Comforter, and at Me, your Friend and Saviour."

He is saying, "The time is short for making your decision as to whom you will serve. I am coming quickly— sooner that you think! I love you so much!"

Come: for All Things Are Now Ready

> . . . A certain man made a great supper, and bade
> many: And sent his servant at supper time to say
> to them that were bidden, Come; for all things
> are now ready. And they all with one consent
> began to make excuse . . . . Then the master of
> the house being angry said to his servant, Go out
> quickly into the streets and lanes of the city, and
> bring in hither the poor, the maimed, and the
> halt, and the blind . . . . compel them to come in,
> that my house may be filled.
>
> Luke 14:16–18, 21, 23

JUST AS IN MY childhood recollections, our heavenly Father has hidden many "goodies" under His banquet plates! Most of them are labeled LESSONS YOU NEED TO LEARN. And all of them are taught when He is ready. He was ready in 1978.

The Lesson

Our TBN volunteers arrived joyfully in Puerto Rico ready to hold huge rallies in the great auditorium in San Juan. The English- and Spanish-speaking evangelists were all "prayed up," and the musicians had tuned up. We had prayed for months that our crusade would lead thousands to the Lord. After all, we were "sacrificing" much time and energy to fly from the comforts of southern California to carry the Good News to those uttermost parts.

It is one thing to be *loved* by the Lord, another to be *led* by Him. We had gotten out in front of Him, which is against His rule—obedient sheep *follow* the leader. As our Shepherd, He must now set us straight—to His glory. He alone knew there existed an unfilled need in San Juan. He would show us—*His* way.

His lesson started with cloudbursts which deluged the island for several days until our arrival. It stopped raining that very day. We had prayed for good weather to permit the crowds to collect. Beneath the headline which announced GOVERNOR DECLARES NATIONAL DISASTER, we read that most roads were under water, hundreds of homes were caving in or sliding down rural hillsides, and that traffic was slowed to a crawl.

Our auditorium "crowd" turned out to be ourselves plus the loyal friends of the local choirs who were providing the music. Marooned islanders had wisely stayed home till the roads and mud could dry out. We returned to the hotel that night, perplexed but prayerful. Our fifty partners requested direction, and the Spirit spoke with a word of knowledge.

"My children, know that I am with thee. The sun will shine, the streets in the city will be dry, and the parks will be filled with hungry souls whom I have led there for

Maybelle touches. Jesus heals. The boy recovers.

you. Go preach and teach and lay on hands. I am with you."

The Shepherd was back in control. Praise the Lord! We could sense that victory would come on the streets, in the parks, along the alleys.

Our crusaders shifted gears. Instead of big meetings, we would have little talks—one to one—under trees, in doorways, at bus stops, in bars, and alongside park benches. We would let the Shepherd lead us to ones He had selected for a blessing. And He did.

The weekend was exciting. The Lord had already made it totally clear that He was eager to return to this distressed earth. Now He was showing us that we were to go into the highways and byways to find the "lost sheep" outside of big auditoriums or even churches and to invite

them one-on-one to accept Jesus' love. He had already
arranged that they would be there.

The Wonders of Witnessing

You are invited to look over my shoulder as we leave
in beautiful sunshine for the steaming city park. It is already teeming with happy families seeking joy. We have
a special brand for them today—the joy of Jesus!

Our sound system and TV equipment were novel
enough to attract the children away from the popcorn
cart, and right on their heels followed their parents.

Dejected loners followed more slowly, compelled by
bored curiosity. With its tempting beat the amplified gui-
tar flung a Spanish chorus of praise across the park:
"Christo te amo, Gloria a Dios. . . ." We invited our amigos
to let Jesus heal their many hurts.

The first man wanted to get rid of his demon that
forced him to hate others. At the name of Jesus, that imp
fled. A child was deaf until someone said, "Jesus, heal!" A
young girl sobbed, "Save me, Jesus, from my sin. Make
me Your child." Joy flooded her face. A tough guy had
sauntered to the edge of the crowd in initial disdain.
Suddenly, he too sobbed and repeated the sinner's
prayer.

Children came running for the little "Bibles" of Spanish verses about Jesus' plan of salvation. "Look, Mommy,
tell me what it says," each one was begging with eyes
sparkling with eager joy. "I can see since that lady
touched me," exclaimed a surprised teenager. "My stom-

An amazed crowd collects in the park, to witness the power of Jesus release a demon from a "mean man who made trouble."

Discouraged tough guys find that Jesus is ready to help when they ask Him to take over.

achache is gone. Where did it go?" asked a little girl who was tugging at her weeping mother's skirt.

The next day we were back on the streets. Paul and Jan led the English-speaking partners in and out of stores and bars while the Spanish partners spoke with loafers on benches and under trees. Almost everyone wanted to hear about this Jesus who gave hope and healed. They eagerly asked God to save their souls, while there was yet time.

One expressionless man was suspicious: "God couldn't love me, senora. I just left prison today for killing a man, and I'm headed to shoot the lawyer who sent me there!"

"But Jesus loved you even before you killed," replied the worker. "You need love now more than ever! Take it *now!*"

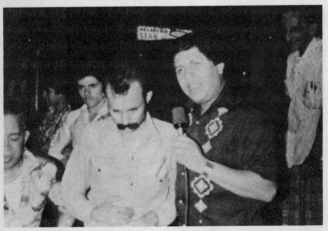

First day out of prison, excon finds Jesus a better answer than vengeance. Manuel explains what this miracle of God's love can do for a former murderer.

His chin quivered and tears started: "Forgive me, Lord. I've been running too long. Save me!"

A sullen lad sat withdrawn on a bench. He wouldn't reply to our partner's query. He couldn't. Three years ago his throat had been cut in a street brawl, severing his vocal cords. His last sound had been a scream. And now a lady was pointing to words in a Spanish Bible: "Thy faith hath made thee whole." She tapped over his heart as she told him, "God in heaven wants to come into your heart." She touched his throat: "He can heal you." The youth nodded and took a breath. Like a small explosion he blurted, "Jesus!" Joyous words poured from his recreated cords. Jesus had ended the silence.

The amazed crowd of onlookers pressed forward. Their bars of resistance were now down. One by one they accepted Jesus' touch of love and healing. It was a

Another miracle! A man says, "Jesus," his first word for years since his throat was slit in a gang fight.

long afternoon, and a strange one for San Juan's street people who had found a new street to travel.

God gave me a special treat. At a storefront mission, I was asked to tell about the heaven and hell which Jesus had shown me. The interpreter had hardly repeated the altar call when a teenage girl rushed to the platform. "Please pray for me, doctor," she said through the interpreter. "Jesus has been standing beside you all the time you were talking, and He was pointing at me to come to Him. I never believed that He was real till tonight. I love Him now. *Gloria a Dios!*" The tears flowed. You may say, "What's one girl amount to, out of all the hundreds in Puerto Rico?" I would reply, "Jesus picked her out personally, and that's enough for me." He has the answer in His Book up there.

The Lessons We Learned

These truths for us in these closing days of our generation are quite clear now. Jesus is saying again and again:

- Seek Me while there is yet time
- Behold, I come quickly
- Pray without ceasing that My will be done
- Forgive others as I have forgiven you
- After the Holy Spirit has come upon you, go teach, preach, lay on hands, cast out devils
- Follow Me, I know My sheep
- Trust Me; I am the Way, the Truth, the Life
- I go to prepare a place for you
- Come: for all things are now ready

He has taught much more in our travels—lessons for every day everywhere. He showed His unchanging right and power to be the Sheperd now just as He was in days of old. He repeated His promise of Exodus 23:20: "Behold, I send an Angel before thee, to keep thee in the way, and to bring thee into the place which I have prepared."

When things go wrong in the lives of believers, it simply means that we were headed for thorns and thistles. With a little chastening here and a little prodding there, our faithful Caretaker is pointing us to His green pastures. How do we know? Through prayer! (*See* Psalms 23:1, 2.)

His Word About Prayer

We are learning that prayer is the key God made whereby we release His self-imposed restraint to bestow upon us His "layaways," that is, His power, peace, patience, wisdom, gifts, and fruits. *Until we pray,* God, by His own decision, cannot fulfill His promises to us— whether temporal or spiritual—nor fulfill prophecies on time. " . . . ye have not, because ye ask not" (James 4:2).

Jesus astounded His disciples by stating unexpectedly:

> Hitherto have ye asked nothing in my name: ask, and ye shall receive, that your joy may be full.
>
> John 16:24

Then He illustrated to them that even their Messiah had to pray to the Father to release the promises and gifts on deposit in heaven:

"Glorify thy Son. . . ."

"I pray for them that thou hast given me. . . ."

"Keep those whom thou hast given me. . . ."

"Keep them from evil. . . ."

"Sanctify them through thy truth. . . ."

"I pray . . . that they all may be one. . . ."

Father, I will that they also . . . be with me where I am, that they may behold my glory, which thou hast given me. . . .

see John 17:1–24

It has taken centuries for this truth to sink in, that God so loves us that He has made prayer *the* power that moves Him to release faith and gifts to His children upon their request. " . . . God hath dealt to every man the measure of faith" (Romans 12:3). He measures it out to us according to our needs, but again only upon request—*prayer.*

He has had all the answers ready for delivery—wrapped and waiting—since eternity began. Although He could distribute them anytime He wished, His omniscience has placed a restriction upon manifesting His generosity prematurely. He elected to make our prayers a prerequisite for the operation of His will, which is to give us every good and perfect gift, on earth as in heaven. Why? Because faith would not have been necessary, if we had already received everything without prayer. Prayer is fellowship with God, and fellowship is what God craves from us, His children. How simple. How profound. What love. What provision. What a promise:

For verily, I say unto you, that whosoever . . . shall believe that those things which he saith shall come to pass; he shall have whatsoever he saith . . . . when ye pray, believe that ye receive them, and ye shall have them.

Mark 11:23, 24

In Conclusion

God's Word says it all:
Come: I love you.

See 1 John 4:19

If you do not as yet love Him in return, repent:
There is yet a little while, but very little.

See John 7:33

If you know Him only as Christ, make Him Lord too:
God hath made that same Jesus, Lord and Christ.

See Acts 2:36

If you seek victory in life, exercise your faith:
. . . this is the victory . . . even our faith.

1 John 5:4

If you need guidance in your life, Jesus says:
But seek ye first the kingdom of God. . . .

Matthew 6:33

If you are a child of God, Jesus says:
. . . ye shall be witnesses unto me . . . unto the uttermost parts of the earth.

Acts 1:8

If you want the Spirit of God to dwell within you:
. . . pray every where, lifting up holy hands, without wrath and doubting.

1 Timothy 2:8

. . . I will pray with the spirit . . . I will pray with understanding. . . .

1 Corinthians 14:15

Benediction

He which testifieth these things saith, surely, I come quickly. Amen. Even so come, Lord Jesus. The grace of our Lord Jesus Christ be with you all. Amen.

Epilogue

My Prayer

Dear Reader:

You have just shared the story of some of our personal experiences of walking and talking with a living, loving Lord.

We know from experience that He is the answer to your needs as well as ours. None of us can fulfill God's plan for us on our own. It simply does not work that way. Only our Creator has the blueprint.

If you are not sure how to tell Jesus you need Him, we invite you to say these simple words out loud before you close this little book:

> God be merciful to me a sinner! I believe Christ died for me and that His precious blood will cleanse me from all my sin. By faith I now receive the Lord Jesus Christ into my heart as my Lord and my Saviour; trusting Him for the salvation of my soul. Help me Lord to do thy will each day. In Jesus' name I pray. Amen.

With John we join in saying: "These things have I written unto you that believe on the name of the Son of God; that ye may know that ye have eternal life..." (1 John 5:13). Jesus loves you and so do we!